eat out
eat smart

eat out
MARTHA SCHUENEMAN
eat smart

**CHECK THE CALORIES, CARBS, AND OTHER NUTRITIONAL
FACTS ON FAST FOODS AND RESTAURANT MEALS**

CHARTWELL
BOOKS, INC.

First published in 2004 by
CHARTWELL BOOKS INC.
A Division of Book Sales Inc.
114 Northfield Avenue
Edison, New Jersey 08837

ISBN: 0-7858-1904-5

Note from the publisher
Information given in this book is not intended to be
taken as a replacement for medical advice. Any person
with a condition requiring medical attention should
consult a qualified medical practitioner or therapist.

This book was conceived, designed, and produced by
THE IVY PRESS LIMITED
The Old Candlemakers
Lewes, East Sussex BN7 2NZ, UK

Creative Director: PETER BRIDGEWATER
Publisher: SOPHIE COLLINS
Editorial Director: JASON HOOK
Design Manager: SIMON GOGGIN
Project Editor: MANDY GREENFIELD
Designer: JANE LANAWAY
Picture Researcher: ANNA DAVIES
Picture Librarian: SHARON DORTENZIO

Printed and bound in China

Contents

Introduction

Muffins or cupcakes? The calories, fat, and carbs are similar.

How often do you eat out? Is breakfast a bowl of cereal at home, or do you stop at a coffee shop or bakery? Do you buy lunch at the company cafeteria, do you go out for a quick bite with friends, or do you bring a sandwich to eat at your desk? Do you run out to get an afternoon pick-me-up of latte and biscotti? Do you zip through the drive-thru while you're ferrying kids to soccer or ballet, or treat yourself to a nice meal with a drink or two after a hectic week?

If you're like most people, you eat an average of four meals away from home every week—and that doesn't include snacks or desserts. In the United States, more than 70 billion meals and snacks will be eaten in restaurants in 2004.

It's easy to eat wholesome, healthful food when you prepare it yourself—you have complete control over the groceries you buy and the ingredients you use. But what do you do when you're at the mercy of a chef or a line cook?

If your schedule finds you eating most of your meals with your feet under a table that isn't your own, don't despair. It is indeed possible to find good-for-you fare that tastes good.

White wine is a low-cal, low-carb beverage.

Opt for vegetable-heavy noodle bowls.

7

WHAT DOES "EATING SMART" INVOLVE?

If you read the newspapers or watch TV, you may well be confused about what, and how much, you should eat.

The fact is, nutrition is a fairly new science—vitamins were identified only about 100 years ago. Studies in nutritional science need to be performed on people, but because people don't generally live carefully controlled lives in laboratories, research is often inexact.

There are, however, a few constants. At its most simplified, you will lose weight if you eat fewer calories than you burn; you'll gain weight if you eat more calories than you burn.

Choose wisely—and limit portions—to avoid surprises!

Doughnuts and fries have a place in a healthful diet, but it's a small one.

In real life, though, it isn't so simple. If you need 2,000 calories a day, getting those 2,000 calories from ice cream, caramel macchiato, doughnuts, and chips will do your body no favors. You need a diet that includes a variety of nutrient-rich foods.

The average, moderately active man needs between 2,000 and 2,500 calories every day to maintain weight. The average woman needs between 1,700 and 2,000. Growing children need about 1,800 calories, more as they get older—teens may require 3,000. Adults over 50 have slower metabolisms, and may need 1,500–2,000.

Foods get their calories from fat, protein, and carbohydrate. Fat is a concentrated source of energy, or calories—it supplies 9 calories per gram. Protein and carbohydrate supply only 4 calories per gram. (Alcohol supplies 7 calories per gram.)

Because fat contains more than twice the calories of protein and carbs, it's often vilified and blamed for weight gain. But the fact is that there are good and bad fats. Actually, some fats are so good they're known as essential fatty acids.

Most fats are a combination of saturated and unsaturated fats. Saturated fats have been linked to heart disease, especially in people whose diets include lots of refined carbohydrates. Saturated fat raises levels of bad cholesterol, but it also raises levels of good cholesterol. Monounsaturated fats have been linked to reducing the likelihood of heart disease, especially in people whose diets are high in complex carbohydrates. Monounsaturated fats also include omega-3 fatty acids, an essential fat that is thought to reduce the chance of fatal heart attacks.

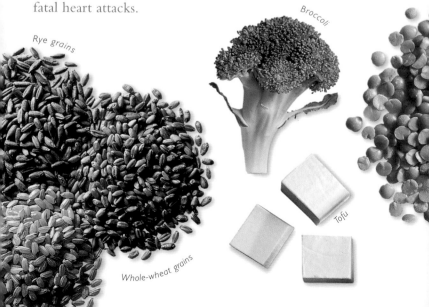

Rye grains

Broccoli

Tofu

Whole-wheat grains

Although saturated fat can be harmful, trans fats can be fatal—they increase bad cholesterol and decrease good cholesterol. Trans fats are found in deep-fried foods and baked goods that contain hydrogenated or partially hydrogenated vegetable oils.

Proteins are often categorized as lean or fatty. Virtually all sources of animal protein contain fat; it varies from extremely low-fat white-fleshed fish to spareribs and bacon, which get nearly 70 percent of their calories from fat. Vegetable proteins, such as tofu and beans, are also lean; they tend to be roughly half protein and half carbohydrate.

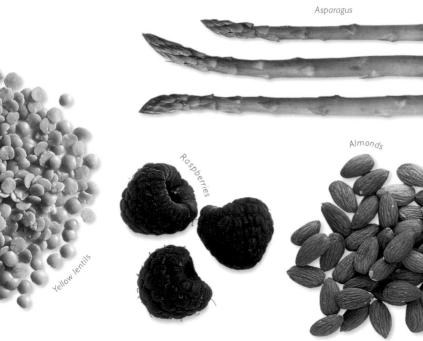

Asparagus

Almonds

Raspberries

Yellow lentils

Carbohydrate and low-carbohydrate diets have been in the news in recent months, but there's still some misconception about whether to eat carbs, which ones to eat, and how much of them to eat. As with fats, there are good carbs and bad carbs. Good carbs, often referred to as complex carbohydrates, are those that are digested slowly and have less of an effect on blood sugar levels; they also tend to be foods that are high in vitamins, minerals, and plant compounds and pigments called phytochemicals—and in fiber. Green vegetables, legumes, nuts, fruits, and whole grains are examples of complex carbs. Refined carbohydrates include sugar, syrup, honey, refined (or white) grains, and foods made from them. They're high in calories, but extremely low in vitamins, minerals, and fiber.

Clear honey

So an "ideal" diet is one that is within the appropriate range of calories for your age, sex, and activity level. It emphasizes lean protein, beneficial fats, and complex carbohydrates to ensure the most nutrients, and it limits refined carbs and harmful fats.

WHAT DOES A "TYPICAL" RESTAURANT MEAL LOOK LIKE?

The sad truth is that most restaurant meals fall far outside the definition of an "ideal" diet. Portions are usually twice as large as recommended, but may be four—or even eight—times that. A box of pasta, for example, provides Nutrition Facts for servings that are about $1/2$ cup cooked, or 2 ounces. If you have it in your head that a "serving" of pasta is about 200 calories and 42 grams of carbohydrate, you may be shocked to learn that a typical restaurant serving of pasta is 4 cups cooked. If you clean your plate, you're eating 1,600 calories

Be careful of dripping-with-oil salads. Even beneficial fats are high in calories!

and 336 grams of carbohydrate—and that doesn't include the sauce. If you order a steak or burger, you're likely to face the same situation. Nutrition experts recommend that a portion of meat be about a quarter of a pound (see Portion Guide, opposite, for what that looks like). At some restaurants, burgers can weigh about double that, and it isn't unusual for steaks to weigh a pound or more!

Even "healthy" foods aren't as good for you as you might think. If you start your meal with a salad, look at the greens to see how many are dark. Romaine, arugula, and spinach are considerably higher in nutrients than iceberg is. Are high-fat, high-carb croutons tossed with the greens? Is there so much dressing that it drips off the lettuce when you lift a bite to your mouth?

And what about vegetables? With the exception of potatoes, most restaurant meals fall woefully short. Those that are served are often liberally sauced, drenched in butter, or are steamed and left bare—virtuous, but not the tastiest.

Although restaurants have come under fire for not offering enough healthful options, you can't always blame them for offering the foods they do. Restaurants create menus in response to consumer demands. If enough people ask for nutritious alternatives, restaurateurs will change their menus to include them.

PORTION GUIDE

If the menu doesn't say, how do you know how much a steak weighs? Short of whipping out a scale or carrying around measuring cups, it's difficult to know how large restaurant servings are. In a pinch, you can use your hand as a guide:

● Your palm (or if your hands are very large or quite small, a deck of cards) = 3 ounces cooked meat, fish, or poultry.

● Your clenched fist (or a tennis ball) = 1 cup

● 1 cupped hand = 1 ounce (of nuts or dried fruits)

● Your thumb tip = 1 tablespoon

Restaurants won't, however, keep nutritious options on menus if no one buys them. If too few patrons order from the "heart-healthy" sections of menus, expect those alternatives to disappear and for less healthful, if not unhealthful, options to take their places.

Dip veggies, not chips, in guacamole for a super nutritious, super tasty, appetizer.

FINDING A BALANCE

For our parents and grandparents, eating out was a special event. Even though we eat out far more often, we might still have the attitude that eating out is an excuse to treat ourselves. If you eat out only on special occasions, indulging is fine. But if you eat out several times a week with such an attitude, you may find yourself packing on the pounds.

Eating well and eating healthfully don't have to be mutually exclusive—even when you're eating out. The most important point to remember is two-pronged: You must limit what you eat, and that means the amount you eat as well as the type of food.

A few restaurants will provide nutrient information, including calorie, fat, protein, carbohydrate, saturated fat, cholesterol, calcium, and sodium content. At the vast majority of restaurants, though, this information is unavailable, at least to consumers. This doesn't mean that a dinner that starts with fried calamari, continues with a 16-ounce steak topped with béarnaise sauce, includes a baked potato topped with sour cream, and ends with crème brûlée is off limits forever. Nor is a Wendy's Triple with everything, Biggie Fries, and a large Frosty.

Brown rice

It does mean that meals like this should be exceptions, not the rule, for several reasons. First, portion sizes at most restaurants are enormous—they're based on the assumption that you expect to get lots and lots of food for your money, and they don't disappoint. They are not based on the assumption that you'll be eating three to five courses and would expect moderately sized servings of each one.

Such menu choices are also high in saturated fat, trans fats, and refined carbohydrates. For the most part, they're also low in the vitamins and minerals necessary for good health.

If you do choose to order several courses, make sure most of them are rich in vegetables and lean protein. Many nutritionists recommend dividing your plate (or your meal) into fourths. Two of the sections should be green vegetables, one should be carbohydrate (preferably whole grains like wheat berries, bulgur, or brown rice), and one should be protein.

Bulgur wheat

Restaurant salads are more than just a plate of greens.

Look for petite steaks, robustly flavored fish like tuna or salmon, vegetable-heavy stir-fried dishes, and appetizers like negimaki or broiled portobellos. If you know you're going to be ordering a decadent dessert, opt for a simple entrée like grilled chicken—or perhaps get an appetizer or a salad and soup. Steer clear of the breaded, the deep-fried, the slathered-with-sauce.

To eat smart when you eat out, view eating out as a part of everyday life, not a special treat. Opt for lean, vegetable-rich dishes for most of your meals and splurge on special occasions, such as your birthday or anniversary.

How to use this book

Eat Out Eat Smart is a practical guide to the best and worst options on menus. Information on calories and other nutrients is available for some restaurants in charts, for others in Smart Choices and Not-so-smart Choices.

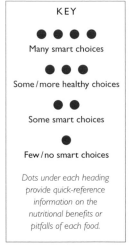

KEY

● ● ● ●
Many smart choices

● ● ●
Some/more healthy choices

● ●
Some smart choices

●
Few/no smart choices

Dots under each heading provide quick-reference information on the nutritional benefits or pitfalls of each food.

CHARTS

● Not all restaurants make nutrition information available. On some pages, you'll find charts that give nutrient amounts for specific portion sizes. In some cases, more than one portion size is given so you can see the difference between a large and super-large order of French fries (for example). Information comes from each restaurant's web site and is subject to change.

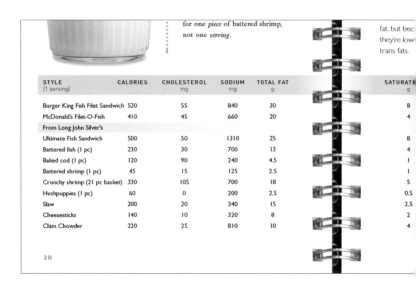

for one *piece* of battered shrimp, not one *serving*.

fat, but bec they're low trans fats.

STYLE (1 serving)	CALORIES	CHOLESTEROL mg	SODIUM mg	TOTAL FAT g	SATURATE g
Burger King Fish Filet Sandwich	520	55	840	30	8
McDonald's Filet-O-Fish	410	45	660	20	4
From Long John Silver's					
Ultimate Fish Sandwich	500	50	1310	25	8
Battered fish (1 pc)	230	30	700	13	4
Baked cod (1 pc)	120	90	240	4.5	1
Battered shrimp (1 pc)	45	15	125	2.5	1
Crunchy shrimp (21 pc basket)	330	105	700	18	5
Hushpuppies (1 pc)	60	0	200	2.5	0.5
Slaw	200	20	340	15	2.5
Cheesesticks	140	10	320	8	2
Clam Chowder	220	25	810	10	4

38

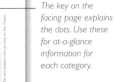

EAT OUT EAT SMART

TACO BELL

• • •

SOME SMART CHOICES

Taco Bell's offerings have always tended to be higher in fiber and lower in saturated fats and cholesterol than most fast-food offerings, thanks to the beans. And they've recently introduced a line of lower-fat menu options.

WHAT'S IN IT?

"Stuft" burritos and Double Decker tacos contain about double the fat, calories, and carbs of regular burritos and single-decker tacos.

STYLE (1 serving)	CALORIES	CHOLESTEROL mg	SODIUM mg	TOTAL FAT g
Fresco Style Grilled Steak Soft Taco	170	5	15	560
Fresco Style Fiesta Burrito, Chicken	350	9	25	1100
Soft Taco, Beef	210	10	25	620
Soft Taco Supreme, Beef	260	14	40	630
Double Decker Taco	340	14	25	800
Gordita Nacho Cheese, Steak	270	11	20	660
Chalupa Baja, Chicken	400	24	40	690
Bean Burrito	370	10	10	1200
Chili Cheese Burrito	390	18	40	1080
Fiesta Burrito, Chicken	370	12	30	1090
Mexican Pizza	550	31	45	1030
Cheese Quesadilla	490	28	55	1150

46

WHAT'S THE BEST?

◉ Steamed or stir-fried vegetables, or Buddha's Delight. With several different vegetables, these are among the lowest fat, lowest calorie, and most nutrient-rich dishes on a menu.

WHAT'S NOT SO GOOD?

◉ MSG (monosodium glutamate). If you're sensitive to the effects of this additive, look on the menu to be sure that the restaurant doesn't use MSG; don't simply rely on a waiter's promise that your dish won't include this flavor enhancer. It may in fact not be added to your order, but MSG is often used in stocks, sauces, and other components of Chinese dishes.

SMART CHOICES

▽▽ Keep an eye out for baked, broiled, steamed, stir-fried, and braised on menus: these are generally low-fat cooking methods.

▽ Steamed vegetable or shrimp dumplings. Tasty, filling, and virtually fat-free, these make a perfect light meal. If you don't think they're enough to satisfy you, order a bowl of soup, too.

NOT-SO-SMART CHOICES

▲▲ Barbecued spareribs. These are among the highest-fat cuts of pork; slather them with a sweet sauce and you'll end up with more than 100 calories per rib.

▲▲ Dry-fried and dry-cooked food. If these terms conjure images of pans devoid of oil, you've brought forth the wrong mental picture. These techniques involve deep-frying in very hot oil. The words sizzling, crispy, and creaky translate to "fried," too.

▲▲ Cold noodles with peanut sauce. Whether they go by this name or are called cold sesame noodles, these are high in calories, fat, and carbs. Pass them by.

The key on the facing page explains the dots. Use these for at-a-glance information for each category.

Not sure what shashlik looks like? Photographs of ingredients and dishes appear on every spread.

Look here for nutritional data about a particular food. If data are not available for a specific food, but the food may contain that nutrient, "NA" is used.

If you're wondering whether a food is good for you —or want to know how you can make it part of a healthful diet—look here.

Where there's too much variation from one restaurant to another to provide nutrient data, look to see whether what you want is a Smart or a Not-so-smart Choice.

CARBOHYDRATE g	FIBER g	SUGARS g
44	2	4
41	1	5
48	3	4
16	0	0
0	1	0
3	0	0
31	2	1
9	1	1
15	2	10
12	1	0
23	<1	8

39

SMART CHOICES KEY

▲ High Fat   ▲ High Calorie

▼ Low Fat   ▼ Low Calorie

▲ High Carbohydrate   ▲ High Nutrition

▼ Low Carbohydrate   ▼ Low Nutrition

FAST-FOOD
RESTAURANTS

FAST-FOOD RESTAURANTS

They're inexpensive, they're familiar, and they're everywhere. Whether you're running errands, walking to campus, or on your way to or from work, the chances are you pass at least one fast-food restaurant.

You don't have to pass them by if you want to eat nutritious food, but you do need to make careful choices—especially if you eat fast food frequently. The predominant method of food preparation is frying, which isn't healthful by anyone's standards.

Please note: like all restaurants, fast-food outlets change their recipes frequently. For the latest nutritional information, ask at the counter or visit the company's web site.

MCDONALD'S

● ●

SOME SMART CHOICES

*S*ave the sandwiches for special occasions—if you eat often at McDonald's, opt for the salads.

TIPS

● Skip salads with "crispy" in the name; go for grilled instead. Pass on croutons: they add calories, fat, and empty carbs.

● Order a kid's meal. These portions are about the size adult portions were 30 years ago.

McNuggets

WHAT'S IN IT?

McDonald's now makes its Chicken McNuggets with white meat, but they're still breaded and fried; they get more than half their calories from fat, and contain as much carbohydrate as they do protein.

STYLE 1 serving	CALORIES	CHOLESTEROL mg	SODIUM mg	TOTAL FAT g
Hamburger	280	30	550	10
Cheeseburger	330	45	790	14
Big N' Tasty	540	80	780	32
Big N' Tasty w/Cheese	590	95	1020	36
Chicken McGrill	400	70	1020	16
Chicken McNuggets (10 pc)	420	60	1120	24
Grilled Chicken Bacon Ranch Salad	250	85	930	10
above w/Ranch Dressing	540	105	1460	40
Crispy Chicken Bacon Ranch Salad	350	65	1000	19
above w/Ranch Dressing	640	85	1530	49
Grilled Chicken Caesar Salad	200	70	820	6
above w/Caesar Dressing	390	90	1320	24
California Cobb Salad (without chicken)	150	85	410	9
above w/Cobb Dressing	270	95	850	18

WHAT'S THE BEST?

● If you want a good-size sandwich, pick the Chicken McGrill. It's about twice the size of a regular kids' hamburger, but it contains only slightly more fat and carbohydrate, and it's slightly lower in saturated fat.

● Watching your sodium as well as your weight? Consider a salad. The Bacon Ranch and Caesar Salads (both without chicken) provide about 10 percent of the recommended daily amount. The Grilled Chicken Salad and the California Cobb Salad without chicken contain less than one-third of the recommended daily amount.

WHAT'S NOT SO GOOD?

● How is it that McDonald's can take foods like honey and mustard, both virtually fat-free, and put them in a Honey Mustard Sauce that gets 80 percent of its calories from fat?

● The Big N' Tasty and Big N' Tasty with Cheese are indeed big—they weigh more than ½ pound each, and have calorie, fat, and carb counts to match. Add an order of fries and a soda and you've got a recipe for disaster on a tray.

Big N' Tasty

SATURATED FAT g	PROTEIN g	CARBOHYDRATE g	FIBER g	SUGARS g
4	12	36	7	2
6	15	36	7	2
10	24	38	9	3
12	27	39	9	3
3	27	37	7	3
5	25	26	0	0
4.5	31	9	3	3
9	32	13	6	3
6	26	20	4	3
10.5	27	24	7	3
3	29	9	3	3
6.5	31	13	5	3
4.5	11	7	3	3
6	12	16	8	3

McDONALD'S
● ●
SOME SMART CHOICES

Apple pie

Fries

*O*ther than salads and fried potatoes, vegetables are in pretty short supply at fast-food restaurants. Most of the beverages and almost all of the desserts are a nutritionist's nightmare, laden with calories, fat, and cholesterol.

TIP

● Skip dessert, or even a dessert-like beverage. McFlurries and Shakes are higher in calories, fat, saturated fat, and cholesterol than the burgers are. Depending on size, they can contain almost twice—yes, twice—as much.

WHAT'S IN IT?

Trans fats. At the time of writing, McDonald's has not switched to trans-fat-free cooking oils. Trans fats are even more harmful than saturated fats are.

STYLE (1 serving)	CALORIES	CHOLESTEROL mg	SODIUM mg	TOTAL FAT g
Small French Fries	210	0	135	10
Medium Fries	450	0	290	22
Super Size Fries	610	0	390	29
Sausage McMuffin	370	50	790	23
Sausage Biscuit	410	35	930	28
Baked Apple Pie	260	0	200	13
M&M McFlurry (12 fl oz)	630	75	210	23
Strawberry Triple Thick Shake (12 fl oz)	420	50	140	12

McMuffin

WHAT'S THE BEST?

● Your smartest breakfast option would be either a McMuffin or a breakfast burrito—the biscuits and the bagels tend to be high in fat and sodium.

● Think small. An order of Super Size Fries is almost three times the size of a small order, and it has almost three times the calories, fat, and carbohydrates.

Shakes tend to pile on the calories, since they contain milk, sugar, and often flavored syrups.

WHAT'S NOT SO GOOD?

● A 16-ounce Nestle Crunch McFlurry weighs in with almost as many calories as a 32-fluid ounce shake. The former has 920 calories, 35 grams of fat, and 129 grams of carbohydrate. A Vanilla Shake has 1,140 calories, 32 grams of fat, and 178 grams of carbohydrate.

SATURATED FAT g	PROTEIN g	CARBOHYDRATE g	FIBER g	SUGARS g
1.5	3	26	2	0
4	6	57	5	0
5	9	77	7	0
9	14	28	2	2
8	10	30	1	2
3.5	3	34	<1	13
15	23	131	2	117
8	11	67	<1	591

BURGER KING

● ●

SOME SMART CHOICES

The good news: Burger King provides consumers with data on the trans fats in their foods. The bad news: You won't always like what you read.

The Veggie Burger is meat-free, but may well have been cooked on the same grill used for meats.

TIP

● Burger King is one of the few fast-food outlets that offers a veggie burger—but it isn't vegetarian. Although the sandwich itself contains no meat products, it may be cooked on the same grills that the beef and chicken are cooked on.

WHAT'S IN IT?

Burger King holds the dubious distinction of having the specialty burger with the highest calories, fat grams, cholesterol, and sodium: the Double Whopper with Cheese weighs in at 1,070 calories, 70 grams of fat, 185 milligrams of cholesterol, and 1,500 milligrams of sodium.

STYLE (1 serving)	CALORIES	CHOLESTEROL mg	SODIUM mg	TOTAL FAT g
Whopper	710	85	980	43
Double Whopper w/Cheese	1070	185	1500	70
Whopper Jr. w/Cheese	440	55	790	26
Hamburger	310	40	580	14
Chicken Whopper	580	75	1370	26
Santa Fe Fire-Grilled Chicken Baguette	350	45	1220	5
Chicken Tenders (5 pc)	210	30	530	12
BK Veggie Burger	340	0	950	10
Chicken Caesar Salad w/Dressing	370	70	1380	20

WHAT'S THE BEST?

● BK has three chicken sandwiches on baguettes: Santa Fe Fire-Grilled Chicken Baguette, Savory Mustard Fire-Grilled Chicken Baguette, and Smoky BBQ Fire-Grilled Chicken Baguette. All have 350 calories, 5 grams of fat, 47–48 grams of carbs— and about half the recommended daily amount of sodium.

WHAT'S NOT SO GOOD?

● Of Burger King's Whopper, McDonald's Big Mac, and Wendy's Classic Single, Burger King's signature burger is the highest in calories, fat, saturated fat, cholesterol, and carbohydrate.

● As with any fast-food restaurant, it isn't just the sandwiches that you need to watch out for. Add an order of fries and a soda and you're looking at a day's worth of calories, fat, and carbohydrate in one meal— and nowhere near enough vitamins and minerals.

The Whopper weighs in at an astonishing 10¼ ounces, and contains calories, fats, and carbs to match.

SATURATED FAT g	PROTEIN g	CARBOHYDRATE g	FIBER g	SUGARS g
13	31	52	4	11
27	57	53	4	11
9	19	32	2	6
5	17	31	2	6
5	39	48	4	7
1.5	29	47	4	4
3.5	14	13	<1	0
1.5	14	47	4	8
5	36	9	3	5

BURGER KING

● ●

SOME SMART CHOICES

If you're looking for a salad, pass Burger King by. Of the major fast-food chains, it has the smallest selection. Your options: Chicken Caesar Salad or Side Garden Salad.

TIP

● Low in both calories and fat, comparatively low in carbohydrate, and high in fiber, Burger King's Chili is also free of trans fats, and provides generous amounts of vitamins A and C.

WHAT'S IN IT?

Burger King's fries are very high in sodium—a King Size order with salt has about three times the sodium of McDonald's largest size; a King order without salt has almost double. McDonald's doesn't supply information on trans fats, but BK's King Fries contain 8 grams per serving.

Fries

STYLE (1 serving)	CALORIES	CHOLESTEROL mg	SODIUM mg	TOTAL FAT g
Small Fries (salt not added)	230	0	410	11
Medium Fries (salt not added)	360	0	380	18
King Fries (salt not added)	600	0	620	30
Side Garden Salad w/Light Italian Dressing	75	0	375	4.5
Chicken Caesar Salad w/Creamy Caesar Dressing	370	70	1380	20
Croissan'wich w/Ham, Egg & Cheese	360	200	1500	20
Croissan'wich w/Egg & Cheese	320	185	720	19
Sourdough Breakfast Sandwich w/Bacon, Egg & Cheese	380	190	990	22
Vanilla Milkshake (medium)	720	125	280	41

Kale

Try to boost your intake of green leafy vegetables and protein at other meals, if you're heading out to eat fast food.

WHAT'S NOT SO GOOD?

● Frozen Minute Maid Cherry. If you choose this, thinking that since it's made with fruit and from the same company that makes orange juice, it's got to be good for you, you'd be wrong. Yes, it's fat-free, but it supplies neither vitamin C nor vitamin A, and a medium contains 113 grams of sugars. That's almost 1/2 cup of sugar, and it's the same as the amount in the Frozen Coca-Cola.

● Breakfast. Burger King's Croissan'wiches, Sourdough Breakfast Sandwiches, and French Toast Sticks are comparable in fat, calories, carbs, and cholesterol to their burgers.

WHAT'S THE BEST?

● Moderation: if you know you'll be eating at Burger King, take care that your food choices for the rest of the day are based on vegetables—particularly green leafy ones—whole grains, and lean protein like broiled or grilled fish.

SATURATED FAT g	PROTEIN g	CARBOHYDRATE g	FIBER g	SUGARS g
3	3	29	2	0
5	4	46	4	<1
8	7	76	6	<1
1	1	9	2	6
5	36	9	3	5
8	18	25	<1	3
7	12	24	<1	3
8	16	30	2	3
27	15	73	1	60

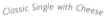
Classic Single with Cheese

WENDY'S

SOME SMART CHOICES

W*endy's offers several salads to choose from, and like most fast-food restaurants, theirs can be customized with a variety of dressings.*

WHAT'S IN IT?

Wendy's salads include more than just iceberg lettuce and some shredded carrot. Their greens include romaine and baby lettuces, as well as cucumbers, onions, tomatoes, and carrots. Romaine lettuce contains six times the vitamin C of iceberg.

WHAT'S THE BEST?

● If you're craving fries, Wendy's is a better alternative to Burger King. Although they're still not the smartest option on the menu, Wendy's fries are lower in fat, saturated fat, and trans fats than Burger King's (McDonald's doesn't provide trans-fat information).

● Skip the crispy rice noodles, honey-roasted pecans, and garlic croutons on your salad; the roasted almonds are a much better choice.

STYLE (1 serving)	CALORIES	CHOLESTEROL mg	SODIUM mg	TOTAL FAT g
Jr. Hamburger	270	30	620	9
Big Bacon Classic	580	95	1430	29
Grilled Chicken Sandwich	300	55	730	6
Spicy Chicken Sandwich	430	60	1220	14
Baked Potato w/Sour Cream & Chives	340	15	40	6
Chili, small	200	35	870	5
French Fries, medium	390	0	340	17
French Fries, Great Biggie	530	0	450	23
Homestyle Chicken Strips	410	60	1470	18
Mandarin Chicken Salad w/Oriental Sesame Dressing	440	50	1300	22
Mandarin Chicken Salad w/Dressing, Crispy Rice Noodles & Roasted Almonds	630	50	1540	35

Taco salad

WHAT'S NOT SO GOOD?

● The Taco Supreme Salad. Made with chili, greens, and Cheddar, it isn't so bad on its own, but load it with sour cream and taco chips and you've almost doubled the calories, fat, and carbs.

● Double and Triple burgers. Each patty adds 200 calories, 14 grams of fat (6 of which are saturated), and 65 milligrams of cholesterol. Stick with the Classic Single and order a salad if you're still hungry.

TIPS

● If you're following a low-fat diet, baked potatoes or chili are better choices than burgers or salads with full-fat dressing.

● More concerned with controlling your carbs? A Caesar Side Salad—without croutons—or a Spring Mix or Chicken BLT Garden Sensations Salad with blue-cheese dressing are your best bets.

● Hungry? From a nutritional standpoint, you're better off ordering two Jr. Hamburgers than one Big Bacon Classic.

SATURATED FAT g	PROTEIN g	CARBOHYDRATE g	FIBER g	SUGARS g
3.5	15	34	2	7
12	33	45	3	11
1.5	24	36	2	8
2.5	28	47	3	6
3.5	8	62	7	3
2	17	21	5	5
3	4	56	6	0
4.5	6	75	8	1
3.5	28	33	0	0
3.5	22	36	3	29
4.5	29	50	5	31

ARBY'S

● ● ●

SOME HEALTHFUL OPTIONS

Y*ou won't find burgers at Arby's, but the chain has expanded far beyond its original concept of roast-beef sandwiches, to offer chicken, turkey, ham, and BLTs.*

A multi-grain bun is a gesture toward healthy eating.

WHAT'S IN IT?

Arby's offers a multi-grain bun, but most of the grain is wheat. Oats, rye, and barley are included, but comprise less than 2 percent of the roll.

WHAT'S THE BEST?

● Arby's roast-beef offerings tend to be lower in calories, fat, protein, carbs, and cholesterol than their chicken sandwiches; comparable in calories; and lower in fat and sodium than the Turkey Club Salad and Chicken Finger Salad.

● The Caesar Salad. Without the chicken, it's an excellent side-dish alternative to fries or Jalapeno Bites.

TIP

● Skip the extra sauces. They're high in sugar and sodium.

STYLE (1 serving)	CALORIES	CHOLESTEROL mg	SODIUM mg	TOTAL FAT g
Junior Roast Beef	310	70	740	13
Arby's Melt w/Cheddar	340	70	890	15
Arby-Q	360	70	1530	14
Chicken Breast Fillet	540	90	1160	30
French Dip	440	100	1680	18
Turkey Sub	630	100	2170	37
Market Fresh Roast Turkey, Ranch & Bacon	880	155	2320	44
Grilled Chicken Caesar (w/o dressing)	230	80	920	8
above w/Caesar dressing	540	85	1340	42
Chicken Finger Salad (w/o dressing)	570	65	1300	34
above w/Ranch Dressing	860	90	1880	64

Filled sandwich

WHAT'S NOT SO GOOD?

● The Market Fresh Sandwiches. They're huge, weighing in at around 3/4 pound, and have the calories, fat, sodium, and carb counts to match.

● Two of the Market Fresh Salads. The Turkey Club and Chicken Finger Salad are considerably higher in fat than the beef sandwiches. If you think that a bowl of vegetables would at least provide fiber, think again: They're within a gram or two of most of the sandwiches.

Caesar salad, with its combination of crisp lettuce and Parmesan cheese, makes a good side-dish choice.

SATURATED FAT g	PROTEIN g	CARBOHYDRATE g	FIBER g	SUGARS g
4.5	16	34	2	NA
5	16	36	2	NA
4	16	40	2	NA
5	24	47	2	NA
8	28	42	2	NA
9	26	51	2	NA
10	48	74	5	NA
3.5	33	8	3	NA
8.5	34	9	3	NA
9	30	39	3	NA
14	31	42	3	NA

KFC

● ●

SOME SMART CHOICES

Even though "fried" is no longer part of KFC's name, just about every entrée on the menu is. But beware: the single worst item on the menu is actually baked.

WHAT'S IN IT?

Ounce for ounce, chicken breast is leaner than chicken drumsticks, but you'll get less fat if you order a drumstick. Why? It's a smaller portion.

Original Recipe Thigh

TIPS

● Remove the skin from your chicken and you'll reduce the calories, total fat, saturated fat, carbs, and sodium.

● Steer clear of the popcorn chicken—by weight, it's higher in fat, calories, and carbohydrate than the same-size portion of an Extra Crispy Thigh, with more breading on its smaller pieces.

STYLE (1 serving)	CALORIES	CHOLESTEROL mg	SODIUM mg	TOTAL FAT g
Original Recipe Breast	380	145	1150	19
Original Recipe Breast, skin and breading removed	140	95	410	3
Extra Crispy Breast	460	135	1230	28
Original Recipe Thigh	360	165	1060	25
Extra Crispy Thigh	370	120	710	26
Chicken Pot Pie	770	115	1680	40
Hot Wings	450	145	1120	29
Green Beans	50	5	460	1.5
Mashed Potatoes	110	0	260	4
Mashed Potatoes w/Gravy	120	0	380	4.5
BBQ Beans	230	0	720	1
Triple Crunch Sandwich w/sauce	670	80	1640	40
Tender Roast Sandwich w/sauce	390	70	810	10
Lil' Bucket Fudge Brownie	270	30	140	9
Lemon Meringue Pie	310	40	160	11

WHAT'S THE BEST?

● Mashed potatoes. Choose mashed potatoes with gravy over potato wedges. You can eat two orders of mashed spuds for comparable fat, carbs, and calories.

● Vegetables. KFC offers green beans and coleslaw. Yes, the latter is doused in a sweet dressing, but cabbage is high in several nutrients, including vitamins A and C.

WHAT'S NOT SO GOOD?

● "Crispy" and "crunchy." When you see these words on a menu, they mean the food has high carbohydrate and high fat. Opt for the Tender Roast Sandwich instead.

● Pot pie. This holds the distinction of being the single highest-fat, highest-calorie, highest-carbohydrate, and highest-sodium item on KFC's menu.

A Tender Roast Sandwich is one of the best KFC options, but steer clear of the sauce.

SATURATED FAT g	PROTEIN g	CARBOHYDRATE g	FIBER g	SUGARS g
6	40	11	0	0
1	29	0	0	0
8	34	19	0	0
7	22	12	0	0
7	21	12	0	0
15	33	70	5	2
6	24	23	1	1
0.5	5	5	2	2
1	2	16	1	0
1	2	18	1	<1
1	8	46	7	22
8	35	42	1	3
4	31	24	1	0
4	2	44	1	39
5	5	47	3	36

FAST-FOOD FISH

●

FEW SMART CHOICES

Invariably, fast-food fish is breaded or batter-dipped, then deep-fried. Pickings at any fast-food fish restaurant, whether chain or independent store, are going to be severely limited.

Don't ignore the carbs and fat in condiments like mayo—they all add up.

The classic combination of fish and fries can result in a double helping of fats.

TIPS

● Condiments count. If you're watching your fat intake, pass on the mayo or tartar sauce. Keeping an eye on your carbs? Cut the ketchup.

● If you request nutritional information from a restaurant, pay attention to portion sizes. Some charts give information for one *piece* of battered shrimp, not one *serving*.

STYLE (1 serving)	CALORIES	CHOLESTEROL mg	SODIUM mg	TOTAL FAT g
Burger King Fish Filet Sandwich	520	55	840	30
McDonald's Filet-O-Fish	410	45	660	20
From Long John Silver's				
Ultimate Fish Sandwich	500	50	1310	25
Battered fish (1 pc)	230	30	700	13
Baked cod (1 pc)	120	90	240	4.5
Battered shrimp (1 pc)	45	15	125	2.5
Crunchy shrimp (21 pc basket)	330	105	700	18
Hushpuppies (1 pc)	60	0	200	2.5
Slaw	200	20	340	15
Cheesesticks	140	10	320	8
Clam Chowder	220	25	810	10

WHAT'S IN IT?

Fish fillets are deep-fried, and that means hydrogenated oils—and trans fats. Fish sandwiches rival burgers in fat, saturated fat, cholesterol, and carbohydrate content.

WHAT'S THE BEST?

● If baked fish is on the menu, it's your smartest choice. As a general rule, it'll have about half the calories, less than half the fat, and will often be free of carbs as well. And because it isn't deep-fried, it'll have far fewer trans fats (if it's prepared with margarine, it will have some).

● Captain D's. Some of the outlets in this chain offer broiled entrées. They're still made with fat, but because they aren't fried, they're lower in total fat and trans fats.

WHAT'S NOT SO GOOD?

● Hushpuppies. Each one can pack up to 60 calories, 3 grams of fat, 10 grams of carbohydrate, and little, if any, vitamins and minerals—and who stops at one? Coleslaw and corn at least provide some complex carbs, fiber, and vitamins.

Filet-O-Fish

SATURATED FAT g	PROTEIN g	CARBOHYDRATE g	FIBER g	SUGARS g
8	18	44	2	4
4	15	41	1	5
8	20	48	3	4
4	11	16	0	0
1	22	0	1	0
1	2	3	0	0
5	12	31	2	1
0.5	1	9	1	1
2.5	1	15	2	10
2	4	12	1	0
4	9	23	<1	8

DOMINO'S

● ●

SOME SMART CHOICES

Bell peppers

Sliced mushrooms

Pizza can be one of the smartest fast-food options— or one of the worst. Stick with thin-crust pizzas and load up on vegetables.

Onion

Olives

Olives

Vegi Feast toppings sound nutritious, but watch the amount of cheese you have on top.

TIP

● Did you know? Instead of ordering extra cheese, you can order *half* the cheese. Make it clear that you want half as much cheese on the entire pie, though, rather than the usual amount on half your pizza. You'll cut the calories, fat, and carbs considerably.

STYLE (2 slices)	CALORIES	CHOLESTEROL mg	SODIUM mg	TOTAL FAT g
Hand Tossed Cheese (12")	375	23	776	11
Hand Tossed Cheese (14")	516	32	1080	15
Deep Dish Cheese (12")	462	30	1123	22
Deep Dish Cheese (14")	677	41	1575	30
MeatZZa Feast (12")	560	64	1463	26
MeatZZa Feast (14")	753	85	1947	35
Deluxe Feast (12")	465	40	1063	18
Deluxe Feast (14")	627	53	1432	24
Vegi Feast (12")	439	34	987	16
Vegi Feast (14")	604	47	1369	22

Mozzarella

WHAT'S IN IT?

Domino's Vegi Feast isn't as nutritious as its name might lead you to believe. It's topped with bell peppers, onions, mushrooms, and olives—not the most nutrient-dense vegetables—and extra cheese.

WHAT'S THE BEST?

● Simplicity. Steer clear of multiple-topping extravaganzas, stuffed crusts, and anything advertised as supreme, extra, deluxe, "the works," or for lovers of a particular topping or category of toppings. These invariably translate to high calories, high fat, and high carbohydrate.

● Blotting. If you're a pepperoni lover, you know that this sausage stands head and shoulders above other meat toppings in giving your pizza a layer of grease. Use paper napkins to blot up as much as possible. Both your heart and your weight will thank you.

WHAT'S NOT SO GOOD?

● Some side dishes. Pizza is basically bread and cheese. So why order cheesy bread or garlic knots as an accompaniment? If you know that a slice or two of pizza won't fill you, get a salad on the side.

● Tomato sauce. Not that there's anything wrong with it, but don't count on this as a serving of vegetables. The typical pizza has about 1/2 cup of sauce on it. If you eat one-fourth of the pie, you're getting a mere 2 tablespoons of sauce.

SATURATED FAT g	PROTEIN g	CARBOHYDRATE g	FIBER g	SUGARS g
5	15	55	3	5
7	21	75	4	6
8	19	56	3	6
11	26	80	5	9
11	26	57	3	5
15	35	78	5	7
8	19.5	57	3	5
10	26	78	5	7
7	19	57	4	5
10	27	78	5	7

PIZZA HUT

● ●

SOME SMART CHOICES

Pizza Hut has added a Fit 'N Delicious line of pies to its menu. They're lower in calories, fat, carbs, and sodium than nearly everything else on offer.

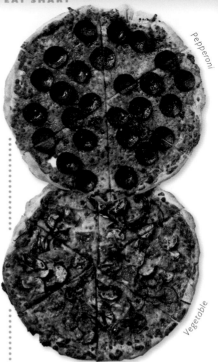

Pepperoni

Vegetable

TIP

● Pizza Hut plays fast and loose with the nutritional information for its Personal Pan Pizzas. Pizza Hut gives it by the slice, not by the pizza.

Opt for Fit 'N Delicious or Thin 'N Crispy pizzas.

STYLE (1 slice)	CALORIES	CHOLESTEROL mg	SODIUM mg	TOTAL FAT g
Pepperoni pizzas:				
Medium Pan	290	25	560	15
Medium Pan, Pepperoni Lover's	340	40	700	19
Medium Hand-Tossed	250	25	570	9
Medium Thin 'N Crispy	210	25	550	10
14" Stuffed Crust	370	45	970	15
16" Extra Large	430	45	1130	17
Personal Pan	170	15	340	8
P'Zone (½ P'Zone)	610	55	1280	22
Other menu items				
Veggie Lover's Personal Pan	150	10	280	6
Chicken Supreme Stuffed Crust	380	40	1020	13
Ham, Red Onion & Mushroom Fit 'N Delicious (12")	160	15	470	4.5
Meat Lover's Hand-Tossed (14")	280	35	710	12

WHAT'S IN IT?

Stuffed crusts are filled with cheese. You probably expect them to have twice as much fat and calories, but they also have twice the carbs. Stick with the Thin 'N Crispy or Hand-Tossed pizzas instead.

WHAT'S THE BEST?

● Pizza Hut's Fit 'N Delicious, Hand-Tossed, and Thin 'N Crispy pizzas are your best bets. Keep the meaty toppings to a minimum, and order a small pie. One slice of a 16-inch pie has more than twice the calories of a 12-inch Thin 'N Crispy.

● See for yourself: the top of the chart below gives information for pepperoni pizzas; the bottom, other offerings from Pizza Hut's menu.

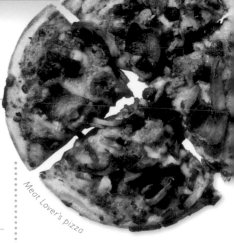

Meat Lover's pizza

WHAT'S NOT SO GOOD?

● P'Zones. Pizza Hut gives nutrient data based on half a P'Zone, a medium pizza folded in half before cooking. If they expect you to eat half a pizza, why is nutrient info for pizzas given by the slice?

● Pan Pizzas. Like the Sicilian Pizza (a specialty item), these thick-crust pies pack on the calories and carbs.

SATURATED FAT g	PROTEIN g	CARBOHYDRATE g	FIBER g	SUGARS g
5	11	29	2	6
7	15	29	2	6
4.5	12	20	2	6
4.5	10	21	1	5
8	18	42	3	8
8	19	50	3	11
3	7	18	<1	4
11	34	69	3	8
2	6	19	1	4
7	20	44	3	10
2	8	22	2	6
6	14	27	2	5

LOCAL PIZZERIAS

● ● ●

MORE SMART CHOICES

*O*rdering from a local pizza joint or regional chain can give you more nutritious options than the huge conglomerates. The downside is that it's harder to get reliable nutrient information.

TIP

● Some pizzerias offer whole-wheat crusts and use reduced-fat cheese. Ask if your favorite place does—or if they'd be willing to try offering healthful options. Smaller businesses are often more willing to respond to customers' requests than large chains are.

Whole-wheat pizzas make a delicious option and are more healthful, too.

WHAT'S IN IT?

Check the menu to see what vegetable toppings are offered. Spinach, broccoli, and red bell peppers are among the most nutrient-dense choices.

Spina

Mozzarella is a popular topping and combines well with a range of ingredients.

What passes for a slice in one pizzeria may be totally different in size in another pizza parlor.

WHAT'S THE BEST?

● Margherita. Made with fresh sliced tomato, fresh basil, and mozzarella, this pizza is wonderful when you don't want something heavy (it's perfect during the summer).

● Think beyond sausage, meatballs, and pepperoni. Independent pizza parlors may offer unusual but tasty combinations of toppings.

WHAT'S NOT SO GOOD?

● Portion confusion. Some chains cut a 14–16-inch pie into as many as 12 slices, while other pizzerias cut the same-size pie into eight pieces. If you use nutrient data from one restaurant to approximate nutrients in another restaurant's pie, don't forget to take this into consideration.

SMART CHOICES

As with pizza chains, pass on extra cheese. In fact, order half the cheese—or no cheese at all—and sprinkle your slice with Parmesan.

Experiment. Try toppings like lemon chicken, garlic shrimp, caramelized onion, feta cheese, or fresh minced garlic.

Supplement your meal with a salad or soup. If you have an antipasto platter, go easy on the cured meats.

If you pass on pizza, opt for a simple pasta sauce like marinara. Avoid baked pasta dishes, which are often loaded with cheese.

NOT-SO-SMART CHOICES

Eggplant *parmigiana*. "It's vegetarian, so it has to be better for me than all that meat, right?" Not so fast. Is the eggplant breaded and fried? Is the entrée or sandwich buried in cheese? You may well be looking at the Italian-food equivalent of a Whopper.

Individual pizzas. Unless they're small—8 inches at the largest—and thin-crust, personal pizzas are loaded with fat and carbs.

Barbecue and bacon. If you're trying new toppings, pass on those that include bacon or barbecued food. The first is high in nitrates, the second in sugar.

TACO BELL

● ●

SOME SMART CHOICES

Taco Bell's offerings have always tended to be higher in fiber and lower in saturated fats and cholesterol than most fast-food offerings, thanks to the beans. And they've recently introduced a line of lower-fat menu options.

WHAT'S IN IT?

"Stuft" burritos and Double Decker tacos contain about double the fat, calories, and carbs of regular burritos and single-decker tacos.

The beans in Taco Bell offerings provide fiber and protein—but go easy on the cheese.

STYLE (1 serving)	CALORIES	CHOLESTEROL mg	SODIUM mg	TOTAL FAT g
Fresco Style Grilled Steak Soft Taco	170	5	15	560
Fresco Style Fiesta Burrito, Chicken	350	9	25	1100
Soft Taco, Beef	210	10	25	620
Soft Taco Supreme, Beef	260	14	40	630
Double Decker Taco	340	14	25	800
Gordita Nacho Cheese, Steak	270	11	20	660
Chalupa Baja, Chicken	400	24	40	690
Bean Burrito	370	10	10	1200
Chili Cheese Burrito	390	18	40	1080
Fiesta Burrito, Chicken	370	12	30	1090
Mexican Pizza	550	31	45	1030
Cheese Quesadilla	490	28	55	1150

Flour tortillas are lower in fat, but higher in carbs, than corn tortillas.

WHAT'S THE BEST?

● Taco Bell now offers 15 items with fewer than 10 grams of fat. You need to be sure you specify that you want a lower-fat item, though: The regular Beef Gordita Baja packs 430 calories and 19 grams of fat. The lower-fat alternative? Only 250 calories and 9 grams of fat.

WHAT'S NOT SO GOOD?

● Taco Salad. If you order it with the edible, deep-fried taco shell bowl, you're adding 370 calories, 21 grams of fat, and 40 grams of carbohydrate.

TIPS

● You're ahead of the game when you order two Tacos instead of one Double Decker. Two regular tacos still contain fewer calories and less carbs and sodium than one Double Decker.

● If you're looking to lower your fat intake, ask if your menu choice is available Fresco Style. Fiesta Salsa is substituted for sauce or cheese.

SATURATED FAT g	PROTEIN g	CARBOHYDRATE g	FIBER g	SUGARS g
1.5	11	21	2	3
2	16	49	4	4
4.5	10	21	2	2
7	11	22	3	3
5	15	39	6	3
3	14	30	2	7
6	17	30	2	4
3.5	14	55	8	4
9	16	40	3	3
3.5	18	48	3	4
11	21	46	7	3
13	19	39	3	4

SUBWAY

SOME SMART CHOICES

*S*ubway holds the distinction of having some of the most healthful fast-food options and some of the least healthful—particularly if you're watching your sodium.

WHAT'S IN IT?

With 10 low-fat sandwiches, 6 low-fat salads, 2 low-carb wraps, and a large selection of soups, Subway has options for nearly every eating plan.

Thanks to the tomato sauce, Chicken Pizziola supplies a whopping 45 percent of the Daily Value for vitamin C.

STYLE (1 serving)	CALORIES	CHOLESTEROL mg	SODIUM mg	TOTAL FAT g
6" Subway Club	320	35	1300	6
Turkey Breast on Deli Round	220	15	730	3.5
6" Subway Melt	410	45	1720	15
Honey Mustard Ham	310	25	1260	5
Chicken Pizziola	450	80	1530	16
Atkins-Friendly Chicken Bacon Ranch Wrap	480	89	1340	27
Double Meat Roast Beef	360	40	1310	7
Double Meat Italian BMT	670	100	2980	38
Roast Beef Salad	120	35	1110	3
Tuna Salad	250	45	870	17
Golden Broccoli & Cheese Soup	180	10	910	12

Tuna salad

TIPS

● Order your sandwich on a Deli Round rather than a 6" loaf for 20 percent fewer carbs. Or choose an Atkins-Friendly Wrap.

● Skip the offerings with "Double" and "Extreme" in the name, and pick and choose carefully among any promotional sandwiches on offer. Some are acceptable, but others are nutritional minefields.

WHAT'S THE BEST?

● If you're not overly concerned with sodium, opt for a cup of Minestrone and a low-fat salad or sandwich. You'll get plenty of vitamins C and A.

● Double Meat Turkey Breast, Ham, Roast Beef, Subway Club, and Chicken. Each one of these supplies less than 10 grams of fat.

WHAT'S NOT SO GOOD?

● Double Meat Italian BMT, Double Meat Cold Cut Trio, Double Meat Subway Melt, and Double Meat Meatball. The first three supply more than a day's worth of the recommended limit of sodium; the last weighs in with 41 grams of fat and 61 grams of carbs—more than any other item on Subway's menu.

● Tuna Salad. If you're keeping tabs on fat grams, this is one sandwich you'll want to steer clear of. Although it certainly sounds healthful, it's one of the highest-fat Classic Sandwiches.

SATURATED FAT g	PROTEIN g	CARBOHYDRATE g	FIBER g	SUGARS g
2	24	46	4	7
1.5	13	36	3	3
6	25	47	4	7
1.5	18	51	4	13
6	31	48	5	8
9	40	19	11	2
3.5	29	46	4	8
14	34	49	4	9
1.5	17	12	3	4
4.5	13	12	3	3
4	6	12	9	4

BOSTON MARKET
● ●
SOME SMART CHOICES

When Boston Market is good, it is very, very good, but when it is bad, it is horrid. And sometimes the choices you think are benign, pack the biggest wallop.

Fresh fruit salad is Boston Market's only dessert to be low in sugars.

STYLE (1 serving)	CALORIES	CHOLESTEROL mg	SODIUM mg	TOTAL FAT g
¼ White Meat Chicken, no skin or wing	170	85	480	4
¼ Dark Meat Chicken, no skin	190	115	440	10
Honey Glazed Ham	210	75	14	8
Meatloaf & Brown Gravy	360	75	920	23
Chunky Chicken Salad	480	110	930	39
Southwestern Grilled Chicken Salad, w/Dressing and Chips	890	115	1100	58
Turkey Tortilla Soup w/Toppings	170	25	1060	8
Green Bean Casserole	80	5	670	4.5
Garlic Dill New Potatoes	130	0	150	2.5
Stuffing	190	5	620	8
Caesar Side Salad	200	15	690	26
BBQ Grilled Chicken Sandwich	830	135	1410	45

Boston Market's Green Bean Casserole is low in calories and cholesterol; or order a side of green beans.

WHAT'S IN IT?

Which is the more nutritious choice: Creamed Spinach or Homestyle Mashed Potatoes with Gravy? Believe it or not, the spuds are lower in calories, fat, saturated fat, and cholesterol, and are higher in fiber, than the spinach. The spinach does, however, have about one-third of the carbs.

WHAT'S THE BEST?

● It's easy enough to eat healthfully at Boston Market—the chicken, turkey, and ham are quite lean and low in carbohydrate. Vegetable sides include green beans, butternut squash, and other steamed vegetables, and the soups are good options, too.

WHAT'S NOT SO GOOD?

● With the exception of Fruit Salad, Boston Market's fruit-based sides are extremely high in sugars. Cranberry Walnut Relish contains 66 grams of sugar—about 1/4 cup—and Hot Cinnamon Apples have 49 grams, or a little over 3 tablespoons.

● Salads and sandwiches. Even without the dressing or chips, the Southwest Grilled Chicken Salad weighs in with 23 grams of fat and 22 grams of carbohydrate. Add the condiments and you're up to 58 grams of fat and 46 grams of carbs.

● Pastry Top Chicken and Turkey Pot Pies. Loaded with calories, fat, and carbs, these could fit into a meal only if you choose your sides very carefully.

SATURATED FAT g	PROTEIN g	CARBOHYDRATE g	FIBER g	SUGARS g
1	33	2	0	1
3	22	1	0	1
3	24	10	0	10
9	23	19	1	3
6	25	4	0	3
11	46	46	7	17
2.5	8	18	2	2
1.5	1	9	2	3
0	3	25	2	2
1.5	5	27	2	5
4.5	5	13	<1	2
11	50	59	2	17

FAST-FOOD KIDS' MEALS

●

FEW HEALTHFUL CHOICES

M ost kids' meals are simply the smallest options on the regular meal—minus the onions and pickles on the burgers.

Junior fries

WHAT'S IN IT?

If you're concerned about what your children eat, limit their exposure to drive-thru dining. Fried chicken and French fries are by far the most popular menu options, and they're full of trans fats. Add the super-sweet condiments and a soda and you're looking at a lot of refined carbs, too.

STYLE (1 serving)	CALORIES	CHOLESTEROL mg	SODIUM mg	TOTAL FAT g
Jr. Grand Slam	397	230	1118	25
Jr. Dippers w/Marinara and French Fries	869	19	1590	44
Jr. Dippers w/Marinara and Applesauce	576	19	1415	27
Frenchtastic Slam	452	311	664	33
Burgerlicious	296	28	368	17
Pizza Party	400	10	1090	15
Dennysaur Chicken Nuggets	190	30	340	13
Macaroni & Cheese	380	25	1240	13
Jr. Fish & Chips	765	44	769	48

Dipping sauce

Dippers

WHAT'S THE BEST?

● Your best bet might be to skip the high-fat finger foods that make up the kids' menus and look for a low-fat entrée. Go for grilled chicken instead of deep-fried, or for baked cod instead of popcorn shrimp.

WHAT'S NOT SO GOOD?

● Soda. One of the leading sources of calories—and sugar—in children's diets, a small soda contains 35–40 grams of sugar, or 9 or 10 teaspoons. If you wouldn't let your kids put that much sugar on their cereal, why would you let them wash down their lunch or dinner with so much?

● Very few restaurants make any nutritional information available for kids' meals. The information given in the table below comes from Denny's restaurant.

Orange soda

SATURATED FAT g	PROTEIN g	CARBOHYDRATE g	FIBER g	SUGARS g
7	17	33	1	2
17	33	81	8	4
12	28	50	5	17
9	19	22	1	3
6	19	22	1	3
3	18	47	7	8
4	9	9	0	0
5	16	49	3	9
9	40	62	4	0

FAST-FOOD DESSERTS

●

FEW HEALTHFUL CHOICES

Yogurt parfait

With few exceptions, the desserts at fast-food and family restaurants are comparable to desserts at most other restaurants.

> **TIP**
>
> ● Your best bet is to have something that fits your needs at home and pass on the desserts while you're out.

WHAT'S IN IT?

Brownie sundaes typically include a brownie that measures 3 inches square—and that's big—plus two or three scoops of vanilla ice cream, a few tablespoons of hot fudge sauce, and at least a ½ cup of whipped cream—and they can include close on 1,000 calories.

STYLE (1 serving)	CALORIES	CHOLESTEROL mg	SODIUM mg	TOTAL FAT g
Denny's				
Hot Fudge Brownie à la Mode	997	14	82	42
Banana Split	894	78	177	43
Chocolate Peanut Butter Pie	653	27	319	39
Carrot Cake	799	125	630	45
Rootbeer Float	280	39	109	10
Wendy's				
Frosty (12 fl oz)	330	35	150	8
Burger King				
Dutch Apple Pie	340	0	470	14
Hershey's Sundae Pie	300	10	190	18
Chocolate Chip Cookies	440	20	360	16
McDonald's				
Fruit 'n Yogurt Parfait	160	5	85	2
Vanilla Reduced-Fat Ice Cream Cone	150	20	75	4.5
Hot Caramel Sundae	260	35	180	10
Baked Apple Pie	260	0	200	13

WHAT'S THE BEST?

● A small—that's about ½ cup—
scoop of ice cream is probably going
to be your best bet in terms of fast-
food desserts. You might even be able
to get it accompanied by some
chopped fruit, or some nuts, but
don't count on it.

WHAT'S NOT SO GOOD?

● Ice-cream sundaes. Whether you
choose a brownie sundae, a banana
split, or a turtle sundae (ice cream,
caramel sauce, and pecans), you're
getting alarming amounts of calories,
fat, and sugars.

Carrot cake

SATURATED FAT g	PROTEIN g	CARBOHYDRATE g	FIBER g	SUGARS g
6	12	147	6	105
19	15	121	6	29
19	15	64	3	45
13	9	99	2	75
6	3	47	0	33
5	8	56	0	42
3	2	52	1	23
10	3	31	1	23
5	5	68	0	32
1	4	30	<1	21
3	4	23	0	17
6	7	61	0	47
3.5	3	34	<1	13

CHAIN
RESTAURANTS

CHAIN RESTAURANTS

When you're looking for a restaurant that's in between a fast-food and white-tablecloth, you'll find myriad options: family restaurants that specialize in pancakes or in buffets; steakhouses; seafood chains; and what the restaurant industry calls "dinner houses"—places like Bennigan's, Chili's, T.G.I. Friday's, Hard Rock Café, and Applebee's.

Many of these restaurants do not make nutrient information available. Some may say this is because it's difficult or impossible to come up with accurate information, due to having different suppliers in different parts of the country, or because each chef prepares your food differently. However, the odds are high that corporate headquarters has guidelines which each chef is supposed to adhere to and that inventory and portion sizes are tightly monitored. After all, the whole point of a chain is that whether you're in Seattle or Miami, you won't find surprises.

FAMILY RESTAURANTS
● ●

SOME SMART CHOICES

From Big Boy and Bob Evans to Roy Rogers and Shoney's, family restaurants often have lengthy menus giving you plenty of options, whether you want pancakes for dinner or a burger at breakfast.

TIPS

● Some restaurants will allow you to order from the kids' or the seniors' menu, no matter what your age is. Portions are smaller on these menus, so it's an easy way to control the amount you eat.

● Scope out the menu to see whether there's a healthful-choices section or an icon marking select dishes.

WHAT'S IN IT?

Rather than what's *in* an entrée, think about what's *on* it. Ordering pancakes? Margarine's high in trans fats, syrup in simple carbohydrates. Getting a sandwich? Condiments like ketchup, honey mustard, barbecue sauce, and salad dressings are high in both, too.

WHAT'S THE BEST?

● A la carte. Rather than order a whole dinner—which may come with soup, and a salad, and a starch, and a side—pick and choose.

● Vegetable plates. Unlike most fast-food places, where veggies are few and far between, family restaurants often have green food on the menu. Some, like Cracker Barrel, have an entrée called a Vegetable Plate; at other restaurants, you may have to order several side dishes.

An array of different vegetable side dishes makes a nutritious choice for vegetarians and nonvegetarians alike.

WHAT'S NOT SO GOOD?

● Watch out for the word "grilled," especially when it's used to describe sandwiches. Find out whether the filling—the chicken or steak—is grilled before it goes between the bread, or whether the bread itself is slathered with butter or margarine and then grilled.

● Barbecue. Whether it refers to ribs, chicken, or baked beans, barbecued foods are high in sugar and, often, high in fat as well. Save these dishes for special occasions.

Grilled chicken is a much better choice than barbecued— although grilled chicken sandwiches are not so smart.

SMART CHOICES

▼▲ Banish the brown. If your entrée allows you to choose from several sides, go for green veggies rather than macaroni and cheese, French fries, potatoes and gravy, stuffing, and baked beans. Even if the broccoli is drenched in a cheese or butter sauce, it's still a better bet than brown, yellow, or white food.

▼▼▲ Whole grains. You could have a bowl of oatmeal doused with heavy cream and sprinkled liberally with brown sugar and still come out ahead of a steak-and-egg breakfast.

▼▼▼▲ Go for the grilled. Chicken, fish, and vegetables, when grilled, can be the leanest, lowest-carb options.

Don't be shy. If the entrée you want comes with coleslaw and fries, ask if you can have yours with greens, or a green salad, and another vegetable.

NOT-SO-SMART CHOICES

▲▲▲ Appetizers. "Breaded," "fried," and "smothered" are words that appear on most menus. Unless you find something that isn't, start your meal with soup or a salad.

▲ Hearty. "Lumberjack," "farmer's," or "country" anything, Dagwood sandwiches, and combo platters are all not-so-secret code for too much food. When you see these words, you can be sure that you're going to get a day or two's worth of calories on a plate—and that's just the entrée.

▲▲ Dinner salads. Believe it or not, these can be higher in fat, calories, and sodium than a cheeseburger. Most have at least ½ cup—yes, four times a "serving"— of dressing. Add marinated meats or ham, fried croutons, and cheese and you're looking at 70 grams of fat.

DINNER HOUSES

●

FEW SMART CHOICES

I f you're looking to eat wisely, then you'll need to be very careful at Bennigan's, Houlihan's, Chili's, and the like.

Craving red meat? Get a steak rather than a burger. Sirloin, for example, is lower in saturated fat than most ground beef, and steak is rarely served on a bun.

WHAT'S IN IT?

The vast majority of dishes at most of these restaurants weigh in at more than 1,000 calories—and that's without an appetizer, dessert, or beverage.

WHAT'S THE BEST?

● Think vegetables. The big advantage of dinner houses is that they have a little of everything on the menu. Look for stir-fried dishes, fajitas with onions and red bell peppers—even veggie burgers. They might not be low in fat, but at least they're rich in vitamins.

WHAT'S NOT SO GOOD?

● Appetizers. One mozzarella stick has as many calories as three strips of bacon and as much fat as two strips. Buffalo wings—even without the blue-cheese dipping sauce—can be higher in fat and carbohydrate than a Burger King Whopper. And onion blossoms? They're comparable to a Whopper with fries.

> ### TIP
>
> ● Ask questions. If you're not sure from the menu how a dish is prepared, ask your server. And if you don't see what you want, ask if the restaurant can accommodate special requests. Some restaurants are happy to make substitutions.

Don't forget that cocktails are laced with calories and sugar— you can't just ignore them in totting up your daily intake.

NOT-SO-SMART CHOICES

▲▲ Burgers. Although they'll never be mistaken for health food, burgers at these restaurants often weigh ½ pound. Add bacon or barbecue sauce, smother it with mushrooms and cheese, and serve it between a necessarily gigantic bun, and you have something that makes fast food look nutritious. How's that for scary?

▲▲ Cleaning your plate. Some restaurants serve 18–20-ounce steaks and chops. Although that weight may include the bone, you're still facing down two or three servings of meat. That doesn't include the fries or garlic mashed potatoes.

▲▲▼ Cocktails. A beer or a glass of wine with your meal is one thing, but pass on the specialty cocktails. Alcohol has 7 calories per gram— almost double that of carbohydrate and protein—and most of the drinks on the menu are loaded with sugary mixes.

SMART CHOICES

▲▲ Skip the sauce. Chances are, it's loaded with trans fats and carbs. Even salad dressings can be high in sugars.

▼▼ Fajitas. Most restaurants give you the fixings and let you roll your own, so that you can customize these to your needs. Skip the sour cream if you're eating low-fat (don't shun the guacamole, though—avocados are high in many nutrients), or toss the tortillas, if you're watching your carbs.

▼▼▼ Moderation. Meeting some friends after work? If you know you'll be indulging in batter-dipped and deep-fried snacks plus a drink or two, be careful that you eat wisely the rest of the day (and maybe the day after).

STEAKHOUSES
● ●

SOME SMART CHOICES

I f beef is what's for dinner, that's fine—just be very careful about what else goes onto your plate.

TIPS

● The same steak can go by many different names—strip steak, New York strip steak, Delmonico, sirloin club, and club steaks are all the same cut . . . but a sirloin steak and a sirloin club steak are not the same.

● Practice portion control. You might not see a kids' or a seniors' section on a steakhouse menu, but many places do offer petite versions of popular steaks. You might not be able to find a 6-ounce T-bone, but a 6-ounce filet mignon or sirloin steak is entirely possible.

Salads go well with steak and count toward the nutrient quota that you need to obtain from vegetables.

WHAT'S THE BEST?

● Trimming. Most beef has plenty of intramuscular fat—that is, fat within the muscles. Cut off the external fat and you'll lighten the calorific load considerably.

● Soup and salad. At many steakhouses, these are included with your meal. Stick with a vegetable-based soup and skip the fried croutons on the salad and you'll be well on your way to meeting your veggie quota for the day.

Steak

Some steaks are more fatty— and fattening—than others, so choose your cut carefully.

WHAT'S IN IT?

Because of its comparatively high saturated fat content, beef has a bad reputation. Different cuts have different fat contents, so it is possible to choose steaks that fit in with a healthy-eating plan.

WHAT'S NOT SO GOOD?

● Cheese fries. A mountain of French fries topped with cheese and bacon, then served with ranch dressing, can be higher in calories and fat than two servings of prime rib— the cut of beef that's highest in fat.

● Chicken salads. There's nothing wrong with ordering something other than steak at a steakhouse, but do read the menu carefully. At many restaurants, the chicken salad starts with greens, then continues with breaded and fried chicken nuggets. Ask for your chicken to be grilled, then cut into strips.

SMART CHOICES

▼▼▼ Looking for a low-calorie, low-carb, low-fat appetizer? Search for shrimp cocktail. Although shrimp is high in cholesterol, the cholesterol in foods has less impact on blood-cholesterol levels than saturated fat does.

▼▲ Sweet potatoes. Order one of these and you'll get 110 percent of your beta-carotene for the day, as well as generous amounts of fiber, vitamins C and E, and iron.

▼▼ Au jus. Ask for this sauce—it's full of flavor and lower in calories than béarnaise or garlic butter.

NOT-SO-SMART CHOICES

▲ Porterhouse and prime rib. These cuts contain more than double the calories and about four times the saturated fat of sirloin and filet mignon (or tenderloin).

▲▲ Gigantic portions. Some steakhouses offer 3- and 4-pound steaks—and some offer prizes to anyone who finishes. Considering that most nutritionists measure a serving as 3–4 *ounces*, you're wise to resist the challenge.

▲▲ Cream-based soup. Soup is an excellent way to start your meal, but order a broth-based one rather than a creamy one.

PANCAKE HOUSES

● ●

SOME SMART CHOICES

*B*reakfast is the most important meal of the day—so be sure that you're getting the nutrients you need to start your day correctly.

WHAT'S IN IT?

The typical cake-and-steak breakfast features a high-fat cured meat like bacon, sausage, or ham, as well as eggs (often cooked in margarine), a couple of pancakes (frequently topped with margarine), maybe some toast (also topped with margarine), and jam or syrup.

WHAT'S THE BEST?

● It's rarely written up to sound delectable or photographed to best advantage, but oatmeal is usually one of the few whole grains on the menu. If you prefer cold cereal, be sure you order one that isn't loaded with sugar.

● A cup of plain yogurt, topped with fresh fruit, provides an astonishing 35–40 percent of your calcium requirement for the day.

Pancakes are an enticing choice—but opt for fresh fruit on top, rather than cream, syrup, or sugary fruit toppings.

yogurt with fruit

Rolled oats

WHAT'S NOT SO GOOD?

● Bacon, ham, and sausage. Bacon's high in fat, ham contains nitrates (compounds that become carcinogenic in the body), and sausage contains fat and carbohydrates. If you want protein, order eggs or a small steak.

SMART CHOICES

▼ Canadian bacon. Made from center-cut pork tenderloin, this is an incredibly lean cut of meat. It's cured, so you won't want to eat it often, but it's the leanest of the breakfast meats.

▼▲ Build-your-own omelets. Most menu offerings are full of meat, cheese, and sauces, but many restaurants will allow you to order specific fillings. Go heavy on the vegetables and light on the meats, particularly if your breakfast comes with a side of bacon.

▼▼ Steak and eggs. Believe it or not, this combo is one of the most low-fat offerings on Denny's menu. It's even lower in fat than the Veggie-Cheese Omelette!

▼▲ Fresh fruit. Ask if you can substitute it for the hash browns that come with your breakfast. Or order it as an appetizer. By eating it first, you'll be sure you're getting plenty of vitamins and nutrients.

NOT-SO-SMART CHOICES

▲▲▲ European-style waffles. These are surprisingly high in fat—and that's without the whipped-cream or cream-cheese toppings.

▲▼ Fruit toppings. Don't drown your pancakes in blueberry syrup and think you're getting fruit! The fruit toppings at most pancake houses are loaded with sugar.

▲▲▲ French toast. If you're avoiding fat, pancakes or oatmeal are breakfast options; if you're avoiding carbs, eggs are a sensible choice. French toast can have 70 grams of fat and more than 100 grams of carbs—before you add butter, margarine, or syrup.

▲▲ Lumberjack or farmer's breakfasts. Unless you've got a forest of logs to split or a field to plow, these breakfasts have way too much food. Steer clear of those dubbed "Grand" and "Tremendous," as well as "Skillet" breakfasts.

SEAFOOD RESTAURANTS

● ● ● ●

MANY SMART CHOICES

Red Lobster is the largest seafood chain, but Legal Sea Foods, Landry's, and other regional chains and independent restaurants have similar fare.

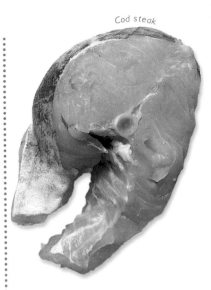

Cod steak

WHAT'S IN IT?

Seafood varies considerably in nutrients. Most white-fleshed fish and shellfish are exceptionally low in fat; higher-fat fish like salmon contain generous amounts of cardio-protective omega-3 fatty acids.

Fresh tuna with ratatouille

WHAT'S THE BEST?

● Obviously low-fat preparations like broiled, grilled, and steamed abound, but scampi and blackened fish dishes are also smart choices. Pass on the drawn butter and tartar sauce (try cocktail sauce instead) and you'll save on fat and carbs as well.

TIP

● Pregnant or nursing mothers, the elderly, children under 12, and anyone with a compromised immune system should avoid eating too much of the large ocean fish, such as shark, swordfish, tuna, and some species of mackerel. These fish may harbor large amounts of toxins like mercury or PCBs (polychlorinated biphenyls).

Baked

Shrimp

WHAT'S NOT SO GOOD?

● Don't be fooled: Fried is fried, whether it's "lightly fried," "batterfried," or "crispy." And most often, frying is done in hydrogenated oils (those that are solid at room temperature).

● Stuffed. Even if a dish is baked after stuffing (shrimp, for example, or clams), it most likely includes bread-crumbs in the stuffing mixture or sprinkled on top to help in browning.

SMART CHOICES

▼▼ Shrimp cocktail. If you want an appetizer, this is the one to choose—mostly because it's one of the only ones that isn't breaded, fried, or drenched with cheese.

▼▼ You-peel-em shrimp. Available at smaller chains and independent restaurants. Shrimp is steamed or boiled in the shell, and you peel them yourself. Because peeling takes time, you eat these slowly. Shrimp is virtually fat-free, so if you skip the sauce, you'll be in great shape.

▼▲ Salmon. If you go just by the numbers, salmon is high in fat—but all fats are not created equal. Salmon is low in saturated fat and high in beneficial omega-3 fats.

▼▼ Broiled foods. Typically cooked with a bit of olive oil and well seasoned with herbs and spices, broiled dishes (including scampi) provide tons of flavor with little fat and no carbs.

NOT-SO-SMART CHOICES

▲▲▲ Popcorn shrimp. Battered or breaded and fried, these are worse than larger battered and fried foods—they have more surface area, so there's more of the bad stuff. Calamari comes into the same category.

▲▲ Biscuits. If you're not concerned about refined carbs, get hard rolls (or ask for whole-wheat bread). Biscuits are much higher in fat than both.

▲▲▲ Fried anything. Although you'll find more healthful options on offer at a seafood restaurant than you will at many other places, you'll still wade through plenty of battered and breaded fish dishes and sides like French fries.

BUFFETS AND BARS

●

FEW SMART CHOICES

Designed to appeal to the value-seeker inherent in all of us, salad bars, buffets, and smorgasbords should be treated with extreme caution.

TIP

● Avoid the buffet whenever possible—who knows how long that stuff has been sitting there? If it's your only option, case the joint first: take one stroll down the buffet to see what's on offer, making a note of what you really love or are hungry for. Then take a second walk down, helping yourself to small-to-medium portions of those few favorite foods.

WHAT'S IN IT?

By definition, you'll find just about everything on a buffet, ranging from breakfast food to meats, pastas and casseroles, salads, cakes, and desserts. Although buffets aren't known for their nutrient-rich offerings, savvy sleuthing should help you identify the best choices.

Soup makes a filling appetizer and is almost guaranteed to take the edge off your appetite.

WHAT'S THE BEST?

● Soup. Start your meal with a cup or bowl of a vegetable soup. It will fill you up so that you're less likely to load your plate and overeat later in your meal.

● Light food. If you're at a salad bar, be wary of heavy foods like pasta salads, coleslaw, cottage cheese (it's usually full-fat), and potato salads. Instead, fill your plate with greens, carrot strips, sliced radishes, tomatoes cucumbers, bell peppers, and other raw vegetables.

WHAT'S NOT SO GOOD?

● Off-peak hours. Foods, especially those that are high in protein, spoil rapidly at room temperature. Hit the buffet during peak hours so that you can be sure the food is as fresh and as safe as possible.

● Dressed salads. Pass on the potato and pasta salads, the bean salads, and even Caesar salads, which are often swimming in dressings.

Coleslaw and potato salad are often smothered in mayonnaise, which is high in fat and calories and is best eaten sparingly.

SMART CHOICES

▼▲ Fresh fruit. Most buffets have grapes, melon chunks or wedges, or a fruit salad. If you're looking to avoid fat, this is your best bet.

▼▼ Look for broiled or roasted meats, prepared simply. Check to see whether the sauce has pools of grease floating on it.

▼▲ Unsauced vegetables. Most buffets groan with cheese-laden casseroles and cream-sauced vegetables, but if the cheese is on the top layer only, you may be in luck. Use the serving spoon to dig deep.

▼ Small plates. The easiest way to limit portion sizes is to use a small plate from the salad or soup section.

NOT-SO-SMART CHOICES

▲▲▲ All-you-can-eat. If you consider this a challenge to get your money's worth, consider that with few exceptions (teenaged boys, professional athletes), restaurants don't lose money on these.

▲▲▼ Most offerings. Breakfast buffets feature pancakes, French toast, bacon, and sausage; lunch and dinner buffets offer fried chicken, pastas, meatloaf, onion rings, fries, potatoes au gratin, barbecued ribs, turkey and stuffing with gravy.

▲ A little of this, a little of that. If this is your approach at a buffet, be sure that "little" really means "little."

OLIVE GARDEN

● ●

SOME SMART CHOICES

O*ne of the most popular chain restaurants and one of the few national Italian restaurants, the Olive Garden has several healthful items on its menu.*

TIP

● Check out Olive Garden's Garden Fare selections if you're watching your fat intake. These have been formulated to obtain no more than 30 percent of their calories from fat. (If you're watching your carbs, though, these entrées have 40 grams of carbohydrate or more.)

WHAT'S IN IT?

Olive Garden's Chicken Scampi isn't scampi in the traditional sense—and not just because it uses chicken instead of shrimp. Scampi usually means brushed with olive oil and grilled or broiled; Olive Garden's dish comes in a cream sauce.

Olive oil is a beneficial monounsaturated fat and is high in vitamin E.

STYLE (1 serving)	CALORIES	CHOLESTEROL mg	SODIUM mg	TOTAL FAT g
Capellini Pomodoro (lunch)	350	5	720	11
Chicken Giardino (lunch)	350	50	1180	7
Linguine alla Marinara (lunch)	280	0	510	6
Shrimp Primavera (lunch)	490	140	820	15
Capellini Pomodoro (dinner)	560	10	1130	18
Chicken Giardino (dinner)	460	60	1180	8
Linguine alla Marinara (dinner)	450	0	770	9
Shrimp Primavera	730	270	1220	25
Minestrone	100	0	610	1
Plain Breadstick	140	0	270	1.5

WHAT'S THE BEST?

● If nothing on the menu strikes your fancy, look for the words *piccata*, *primavera*, *marinara*, and *pomodoro*. The Salmon *Piccata* and Shrimp *Primavera* are good choices. *Piccata* indicates a lemony sauce; *primavera*, vegetables; *marinara*, seafood; and *pomodoro*, tomato.

● Mussels, simmered in wine and a garlic-butter sauce, are an excellent, low-carb alternative to breaded and fried appetizers.

If you see the word "primavera" on the menu, it means that the dish in question will have a vegetable sauce.

WHAT'S NOT SO GOOD?

● As with any Italian restaurant, watch out for words like *alfredo*, *parmigiana*, *formaggio*, and *rustico*. *Al forno* means "cooked in the oven," and although baked dishes aren't always high in fat, this can be a clue that there is a lot of cheese.

SATURATED FAT g	PROTEIN g	CARBOHYDRATE g	FIBER g	SUGARS g
1.5	10	52	NA	NA
3	26	40	NA	NA
1	8	48	NA	NA
2	26	650	NA	NA
3	17	84	NA	NA
3	36	59	NA	NA
1.5	14	79	NA	NA
4	44	84	NA	NA
0	5	18	NA	NA
0	5	26	NA	NA

BREAKFASTS AND DESSERTS

BREAKFASTS AND DESSERTS

If it seems strange to link the first meal of the day with dessert, consider how similar an apple turnover and an apple pie are, or yogurt and dessert. How you start and end your day can have a tremendous impact on both your weight and your health.

Doughnuts, muffins, coffee drinks, cookies, and ice cream will never be considered nutrient-rich, but it's the rare person who swears off them forever, permanently. While none of these foods is really good for you, not all of them are bad.

DUNKIN DONUTS AND KRISPY KREME

FEW SMART CHOICES

unkin Donuts and Krispy Kreme are terrifically popular, and for good reason—doughnuts, muffins, and breakfast pastries are a convenient and surefire way to satisfy a sweet tooth.

WHAT'S IN IT?

If you've been inside a Krispy Kreme store, you know that doughnuts are fried. They also contain fats, so you're getting a double whammy, including trans fats. Doughnuts are high in refined flour and sugar.

TIPS

● There's really no way to make a doughnut, cinnamon bun, or muffin healthful—even whole-wheat and fruity ones are high in fat and carbs.

● Bagels are low in fat, but they can be high in calories.

STYLE (1 serving)	CALORIES	CHOLESTEROL mg	SODIUM mg	TOTAL FAT g
Krispy Kreme				
Original Glazed	200	5	95	12
Chocolate Iced Glazed	250	5	100	12
Chocolate Malted Crème	390	5	180	21
Glazed Raspberry Filled	200	5	125	16
Honey & Oat	340	20	310	18
Sugar Coated	200	5	95	12
Cinnamon Bun	260	5	125	16
Traditional Cake	230	20	320	13
Glazed Custard Filled	290	5	160	16
Dunkin Donuts				
Black Raspberry	210	0	280	8
Chocolate Frosted Cake	360	25	350	20
Glazed Cake	350	25	340	19
Sugar Raised	170	0	280	8
Jelly Filled	210	0	280	8
Whole Wheat Glazed Cake	310	0	380	19

Doughnuts

WHAT'S THE BEST?

● With few exceptions, the simpler, the better. Small cake doughnuts or yeast doughnuts—unfilled, unfrosted, unsugared—are going to be lower in calories, fat, and carbohydrate.

● Doughnut holes. Nutritionally, these are the same as doughnuts, but if you're able to limit yourself to one or two, you'll be able to take advantage of their built-in portion control.

● Raised doughnuts. Nutritious? No, but yeast-raised doughnuts are lower in fat and calories than cake doughnuts.

WHAT'S NOT SO GOOD?

● Jelly- or cream-filled doughnuts, and frosted, glazed, or sugared doughnuts should be saved for once-a-month treats.

● Muffins. No matter how nutritious they sound, blueberry, corn, carrot, banana, and even bran muffins are closer to cake than to nutrient-rich whole-grain foods.

● Do not be tempted by "healthy"-sounding doughnuts such as Krispy Kreme's Honey and Oat, or Dunkin Donuts's Whole Wheat Glazed Cake. They're every bit as high in fat and carbohydrates, and every bit as low in fiber, as less obviously bad-for-you ones.

SATURATED FAT g	PROTEIN g	CARBOHYDRATE g	FIBER g	SUGARS g
3	2	22	<1	10
3	3	33	<1	21
5	4	49	<1	30
4	3	39	<1	21
4.5	3	42	<1	27
3	2	21	0	19
4	3	28	<1	13
3	3	25	<1	9
4	3	34	<1	17
1.5	3	32	1	10
5	4	40	1	15
5	4	41	1	21
1.5	3	32	1	14
1.5	3	32	1	14
4	4	32	2	14

Triple berry muffin

AU BON PAIN
● ●

SOME SMART CHOICES

*D*on't be fooled by the numbers below—croissants are lower in calories, fat, and carbs than muffins and bagels may be, but they tend to be smaller, too.

TIP

● If you really want a healthy breakfast, skip the pastries and breads. Grab the yogurt cup instead.

WHAT'S IN IT?

Au Bon Pain's Carrot Nut Muffin provides a whopping 190 percent of the recommended daily amount of vitamin A—a little more than the amount in 1 cup of cooked carrots— but it also weighs in at 550 calories, 27 grams of fat, and 71 grams of carbohydrate.

STYLE (1 serving)	CALORIES	CHOLESTEROL mg	SODIUM mg	TOTAL FAT g
Asiago Bagel	380	20	740	8
Cinnamon Crisp Bagel	430	0	430	6
Cinnamon Raisin Bagel	330	0	480	1
Honey 9-grain Bagel	360	0	550	2
Plain Bagel	300	0	470	1
Plain Croissant	250	25	340	6
Sweet Cheese Croissant	350	125	340	14
Spinach & Cheese Croissant	250	35	400	9
Apple Croissant	230	20	220	3
Orange Scone	410	125	340	14
Raisin Bran Muffin	480	30	520	12
Banana Walnut Muffin	440	20	450	19
Carrot Nut Muffin	550	60	860	27
Chocolate Chunk Muffin	590	25	480	20
Low-Fat Triple Berry Muffin	290	25	310	2
Pecan Roll	750	15	560	29
Yogurt w/Granola & Fruit (small)	310	10	130	6

WHAT'S THE BEST?

● All varieties of the Yogurt with Granola & Fruit have the same nutritional composition; the small ones are exactly half the size of the large, so aim small.

● Craving a pastry? Opt for the Spinach & Cheese Croissant. It's comparatively low in calories, fat, and carbohydrate, and it supplies 45 percent of the recommended daily amount of vitamin A and 20 percent of your calcium requirement.

WHAT'S NOT SO GOOD?

● Flavored bagels. Once you start adding in fruit, sugar, and cheese, the fat, calories, and carbs can sky-rocket.

● Muffins. These are perceived as a healthful alternative to doughnuts and other pastries, but because of their often-gigantic size, they're higher in calories and carbohydrate and are comparable in fat.

● Pecan rolls. Adrift in a sea of butter and sugar, these contain about a third of the calories you should eat in a day.

SATURATED FAT g	PROTEIN g	CARBOHYDRATE g	FIBER g	SUGARS g
4.5	18	59	3	5
1	11	96	3	25
0	12	71	3	5
0	14	75	6	5
0	12	61	3	5
3	8	44	2	6
8	11	62	2	12
6	10	32	2	5
1.5	6	47	2	19
8	6	62	2	12
2.5	13	90	10	38
2	9	60	3	24
5	9	71	4	40
6	10	83	5	46
0.5	5	61	2	31
7	14	112	4	48
2	10	56	2	36

STARBUCKS

● ●

SOME SMART CHOICES

*K*nown for its coffee, Starbucks also offers a variety of baked goods for breakfast or a midafternoon pick-me-up.

Coffee

WHAT'S IN IT?

A 16-fluid ounce cup of coffee—what Starbucks calls a grande—has no calories. Add whole milk and you're up to 10 calories (2 grams of carbohydrate). Change the coffee to a latte or cappuccino, add more milk and a syrup, and the numbers increase exponentially.

WHAT'S THE BEST?

● Try latte and cappuccino with nonfat milk. Because these drinks contain a greater percentage of milk compared to coffee than a

STYLE (1 serving)	CALORIES	CHOLESTEROL mg	SODIUM mg	TOTAL FAT g
Beverages (all 16 fl oz, made with whole milk unless noted, with no whipped cream)				
White Hot Chocolate	480	55	300	18
Latte	260	55	200	14
Latte (nonfat milk)	160	10	220	0
Cappuccino	150	30	115	8
Iced Caramel Macchiato	270	40	150	10
Chocolate Brownie Frappuccino	370	15	310	9
Mocha Malt Frappuccino	290	15	250	4
Steamed Apple Cider	230	0	20	0
Chai	290	30	120	7
Chai Crème Frappuccino	370	<5	370	4.5
Baked Goods				
Cinnamon Bagel	430	0	570	1
Carrot Cake	430	85	440	25
Oatmeal Cranberry Mountain	430	60	320	24
Chocolate Hazelnut Biscotti	110	25	80	5
Classic Coffee Cake	570	75	310	28
Blueberry Walnut Coffee Cake	340	60	360	18
Blueberry Muffin	380	70	380	19
Crisp Cinnamon Twist	60	0	25	2

regular coffee with milk, they taste richer than a regular coffee.

● Need a nibble? Opt for a biscotti or Crisp Cinnamon Twist. Of all the treats, they're the lowest in calories and carbs; only bagels are lower in fat.

WHAT'S NOT SO GOOD?

● Don't kid yourself: healthy-sounding treats such as Oatmeal Cranberry Mountain and Carrot Cake are just that—healthy-*sounding*. These sweet treats are as high as, if not higher in, calories and fat as any other baked goods.

Carrot cake

● White hot chocolate. With almost 500 calories and more than 60 grams of carbohydrate, this is not the drink to choose if you don't like coffee. Opt for a hot cider or chai instead.

TIP

● Whipped cream atop your drink can add between 50 and 100 calories, almost all of them coming from fat.

SATURATED FAT g	PROTEIN g	CARBOHYDRATE g	FIBER g	SUGARS g
12	17	63	0	62
9	14	21	0	19
0	16	24	0	20
5	8	13	0	11
6	10	34	0	31
6	7	69	2	56
2	6	58	0	48
0	0	57	0	52
4.5	8	50	0	46
1	15	69	0	64
0	13	96	3	14
9	4	46	<1	35
13	7	49	3	22
2	2	15	1	8
10	7	75	2	45
5	4	43	1	30
3.5	5	49	1	28
0.5	0	9	0	4

MRS. FIELDS

●

NO SMART CHOICES

*N*o one goes into a cookie store expecting health food. *Although there's nothing that really qualifies as a smart choice here, some options are definitely smarter than others.*

Chocolate chip cookie

WHAT'S IN IT?

Mrs. Fields web site says that all cookies contain flour, sugar, butter, and whole eggs—which makes it seem like they'd be better than trans-fat-laden supermarket cookies. But then it goes on to say that all cookies may contain partially hydrogenated vegetable oils.

TIP

● If you're a quantity person—if you know one cookie just isn't enough, no matter what its size—order two Nibblers (or get the smallest bag and share it). You'll save considerably on calories, fat, and sugars.

STYLE (1 serving)	CALORIES	CHOLESTEROL mg	SODIUM mg	TOTAL FAT g
Cookies				
Cinnamon Sugar	300	50	250	12
Milk Chocolate Walnut	320	40	180	17
Oatmeal Raisin Walnut	280	40	180	12
Peanut Butter	310	45	260	16
Semi Sweet	280	30	160	14
White Chunk Macadamia	310	35	170	17
Nibblers (2 per serving)				
Chewy Chocolate Fudge	110	10	130	5
Milk Chocolate Walnut	120	10	65	6
Triple Chocolate	110	15	65	6
Brownies				
Pecan Fudge	340	70	220	21
Frosted Fudge	440	80	265	21

WHAT'S THE BEST?

● Infrequent stops. Cookies have their place in a healthful diet, but it's a small one. Save them for a special treat rather than an everyday event.

● Realism. Yes, the oatmeal and raisins and walnuts in cookies provide some nutrients, but the benefits are modest at best. These are still cookies.

WHAT'S NOT SO GOOD?

● Brownies. These are bigger and denser than the cookies, and they have the calories, carbs, and fat grams to prove it.

Brownies and other chocolate-laden cookies are best savored infrequently.

SATURATED FAT g	PROTEIN g	CARBOHYDRATE g	FIBER g	SUGARS g
8	3	41	<1	23
9	4	37	1	26
6	4	29	2	25
8	5	34	<1	18
8	2	40	1	26
9	4	37	<1	25
3.5	1	15	<1	10
3	1	14	<1	9
3	1	15	<1	11
9	4	40	2	30
12	4	62	2	41

SOFT-SERVE ICE CREAM AND FROZEN YOGURT

● ●

SOME SMART CHOICES

Frozen yogurt sounds like a healthier option, but is still high in carbs and calories.

The vast majority of your options at places like Dairy Queen and TCBY are going to be high in carbohydrates and fat; however, some ice-cream parlors may offer sugar-free or fat-free treats.

WHAT'S IN IT?

Nutrient information at many places is given for ½-cup servings—that's 4 fluid ounces—but a medium cup often holds 8 fluid ounces, while a large one holds 11 fluid ounces.

STYLE (1 serving)	CALORIES	CHOLESTEROL mg	SODIUM mg	TOTAL FAT g
TCBY (½ cup, or 4 fl oz)				
Nonfat Frozen Yogurt	110	<5	60	0
No-Sugar-Added Nonfat Frozen Yogurt	90	<5	35	0
96% Fat-Free Frozen Yogurt	140	15	60	3
Nonfat, Nondairy Sorbet	110	0	30	0
Dairy Queen				
Vanilla Soft Serve Cone (½ cup)	140	15	70	4.5
Small Vanilla Cone	230	20	115	7
Medium Chocolate Cone	340	30	160	11
Medium Dipped Cone	490	30	190	24
Small Chocolate Malt	640	55	340	16
Small Chocolate Shake	560	50	280	15
Medium Strawberry Sundae	340	30	160	9
Banana Split	510	30	180	12
Dilly Bar	210	10	75	13
Small Oreo Cookies Blizzard	570	40	430	21
Large Chocolate Chip Cookie Dough Blizzard	1320	90	670	52

TIP

● Pass on the toppings, the mix-ins, syrups, and sprinkles. With the exception of nuts, all are high in sugars and trans fats and have no nutritional value.

WHAT'S THE BEST?

● TCBY's Sorbet Fizz. Made with Diet Sprite instead of regular, this has comparatively few grams of carbohydrates and no fat.

● Small cones. Consider that a small vanilla cone has 230 calories, a large cone 480, and a large dipped cone weighs in at 710 calories.

WHAT'S NOT SO GOOD?

● Before you order that Chocolate Chip Cookie Dough Blizzard, take a look at the numbers below to see if it's really worth it.

● Frozen yogurt. It's lower in fat than ice cream, but every bit as high in calories and carbs. In fact, TCBY doesn't provide nutrient analysis for parfaits, shakes, and sundaes on its web site—only for those foods that are listed below.

Ice-cream cone

SATURATED FAT g	PROTEIN g	CARBOHYDRATE g	FIBER g	SUGARS g
0	4	23	0	20
0	4	20	0	7
2	4	23	0	20
0	0	24	0	19
3	3	22	0	19
4.5	6	38	0	27
7	8	53	0	34
13	8	59	1	43
11	15	111	1	97
10	13	93	1	83
6	7	58	<1	51
8	8	96	3	82
7	3	21	0	17
10	11	83	<1	64
26	21	193	0	143

Chocolate chip

ICE CREAM

●

FEW SMART CHOICES

Regular ice creams contain more air than super-premium ones, so they're slightly lower in both fat and calories.

WHAT'S IN IT?

Haagen-Dazs and other super-premium ice creams have very little air mixed into them. As a result, they're dense and smooth—and very high in fat.

STYLE (1 serving)	CALORIES	CHOLESTEROL mg	SODIUM mg	TOTAL FAT g
Baskin-Robbins (all ice cream is ½ cup or 4 fl oz; drinks are 16 fl oz)				
Mint Chocolate Chip	270	55	95	16
Chocolate	260	50	130	14
Chocolate Fudge	270	50	140	15
Blueberry Cheesecake	270	55	125	14
2-scoop Hot Fudge Sundae	530	85	200	29
3-scoop Hot Fudge Sundae	750	125	280	41
Chocolate Shake, made w/Chocolate Ice Cream	620	105	300	30
Chocolate Shake, made w/Vanilla Ice Cream and Chocolate Syrup	690	130	210	33
Peach Smoothie w/Soft Serve Yogurt	350	5	140	1
Cappuccino Blast	450	45	140	12
Cappuccino Blast (nonfat milk)	210	5	120	0
Orange Sherbet	160	10	40	2
Perils of Praline Low-Fat Yogurt	190	10	105	3.5
Vanilla Nonfat yogurt	150	5	105	0
Haagen-Dazs				
Blueberry Cheesecake	310	120	160	19
Chocolate	270	115	60	18
Peanut Butter Fudge Chunk	340	95	95	23
Dulce de Leche	290	100	95	17
Apple Pie Frozen Yogurt	230	55	70	6
Vanilla Frozen Yogurt	200	65	55	4.5
Chocolate Sorbet	130	0	70	0.5
Zesty Lemon Sorbet	120	0	0	0

WHAT'S THE BEST?

● Kiddie cones. If a small scoop will satisfy you, get a child-size serving. Otherwise, go with a single scoop.

● Ices and sorbets are made with water; sherbets with water and milk; ice cream with cream and milk. The calories and fat content increase respectively; the carbs, too.

WHAT'S NOT SO GOOD?

● Toppings. Cones add calories, but if you're tempted by toppings when you order in a cup, go for a cone.

● Waffle cones. The sole exception to the above rule, these extra-large cones each supply 121 calories, 2 grams of fat, and 23 grams of carbohydrate.

SATURATED FAT g	PROTEIN g	CARBOHYDRATE g	FIBER g	SUGARS g
10	5	28	1	26
9	5	33	0	31
10	4	35	0	32
8	5	32	0	30
19	8	62	0	52
27	11	86	0	74
18	15	81	1	77
21	13	85	0	83
0.5	7	80	3	75
8	6	81	0	79
0	<1	45	0	44
1.5	1	34	0	34
1.5	4	34	1	9
0	6	32	0	31
12	4	30	0	28
11	5	22	1	21
11	7	25	1	22
10	5	28	0	28
4	7	35	0	25
2.5	9	31	0	21
0	2	28	2	20
0	0	31	<1	27

CAKES, PIES, AND OTHER DESSERTS

●

FEW HEALTHFUL CHOICES

*C*an dessert be part of a healthful diet? Yes, as long as it's a small—or infrequent—part.

Apple pie

WHAT'S IN IT?

Almost without exception, desserts are high in fat and refined carbohydrates—and the fat may well be harmful trans fats. Butter or shortening, flour, sugar, cream, and eggs are common ingredients.

WHAT'S THE BEST?

● Small portions are critical. If the sliver you ask for turns out to be a wedge, cut off the part you were expecting and eat that. When you've finished it, set your plate down or put it well to one side.

WHAT'S NOT SO GOOD?

● The more components to a dessert, the more calories, fat grams, and carbohydrates it's likely to have: Cooked apples aren't so bad; add a pie crust and a butter-crumb topping, though, and you've Dutch apple pie—and an additional 300–400 calories.

TIP

● Dark chocolate—in small amounts (about an ounce per day)—can have beneficial effects. Chocolate contains catechins, the same potent group of antioxidants that are found in red wine and tea.

Sorbet

NOT-SO-SMART CHOICES

▲▲▲ Carrot cake. It sounds so healthful, doesn't it? But when it's spread with cream-cheese frosting, it can contain high amounts of calories, fat, and carbohydrate.

▲▲ A la mode. A slice of apple pie can have between 350 and 500 calories in it. Add a scoop—or two—of vanilla ice cream, and you've added another 150–200.

▲▲ After-dinner drinks. If you're planning to order a sweet libation after your meal, then skip dessert. Many liqueurs have as many as 150 calories per fluid ounce, and the typical serving is 1½ –2 fluid ounces.

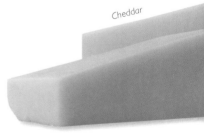

Cheddar

SMART CHOICES

▼▲ Cheese. Studies have shown that eating a sharp, aged cheese after a meal can help to reduce the likelihood of tooth decay. Aged cheeses include Cheddar, Asiago, Manchego, and Parmesan.

▼▲ Fruit. Pass on the poached pears and the bananas foster, and ask for fresh berries instead. You'll get vitamins A and C, plus generous amounts of antioxidants and fiber, too.

▼ Sorbet. Are you craving something cold? This frozen dessert is made with water, not milk or cream, so it's virtually fat-free.

Parmesan

COOL AND CREAMY DESSERTS

●

FEW HEALTHFUL CHOICES

*I*f *you look carefully and choose wisely, you'll find some custards and frozen desserts that provide some nutritional benefit.*

Cheesecake is a sinful dessert: high in fact, low in nutritional benefit, and probably high in sugar, too.

WHAT'S IN IT?

Even though they contain only small amounts of cornstarch or flour, soufflés, puddings, and custards are still extremely high in refined carbs. Sugar is a primary ingredient, and milk may be, too; cream adds fat; eggs add some nutrients, but when combined with the other ingredients, their benefits are diluted.

WHAT'S THE BEST?

● Milk-based desserts like pudding, custard, and mousse can supply generous amounts of calcium.

WHAT'S NOT SO GOOD?

● Cheesecakes are made with cream cheese, a fresh cheese that's extremely high in fat and low in both calcium and protein. Add the sugar and the graham-cracker crust, and maybe a syrupy fruit topping as well, and you're looking at a dietary disaster.

TIP

● If you order a sundae or crème brûlée, ask for two—or more—spoons. Splitting these rich, high-sugar, high-fat desserts is one way to get to enjoy their flavors without doing too much damage to your diet and your waistline.

Crème brûlée is one of the most sugary foods going, so try to share it with one (or more) friends to reduce its impact.

SMART CHOICES

▼ Granita. Similar to a sorbet, but grainier in texture, granita is usually fat-free, and those that are made with fruit may supply some vitamin C. (They contain considerably more sugar and less fiber than the actual fruit does, though.)

▲ Pudding. A wine-glass serving of pudding can supply about 20 percent of your calcium requirement for the day. (It also contains considerable refined carbohydrate, so don't use it as your main source of this important mineral.)

▲ Mousses and soufflés. Though no one would ever mistake these for health food, they may be somewhat lighter than custards or puddings: They get their texture from egg whites that have considerable air beaten into them.

NOT-SO-SMART CHOICES

▲▲▲ Cream pies. Whether you're considering ordering the prosaically named banana cream pie or something as poetical as peanut butter panic or Mississippi mud pie, remember: the crusts often contain butter (even graham cracker crusts); the fillings usually contain cream or ice cream; and the toppings are almost pure sugar.

▲▲ Crème brûlée. This ultra-rich dessert, and its cousins—flan and panna cotta—are even higher in sugars than most custards. Crème brûlée is topped with sugar, then broiled until the sugar melts and forms a brittle crust; flan and panna cotta are prepared in a mold covered with caramel.

▲▲ Sundaes. A small scoop of ice cream is acceptable. Most sundaes, however, involve two or three—or more—scoops, plus toppings like hot fudge, caramel, or butterscotch sauce, whipped cream, syrupy fruits, and chopped candies.

ASIAN
RESTAURANTS

ASIAN RESTAURANTS

The cuisines of Asia resemble one another and overlap somewhat, but each has a distinctive style of presentation, combination of flavors, and method of preparation. Garlic, chiles, soy sauce or fish sauce, fruit or sugar, tamarind or vinegar, and herbs provide the hot, salty, sweet, sour, and bitter elements that most of these cuisines feature.

As a general rule, Asian cooking is low in fat—when it's prepared authentically. Unfortunately, traditional recipes are often modified for Western palates, and fat and calorie counts then escalate dramatically.

Rice is the foundation in most of these cuisines, but wheat—in the form of noodles or breads—is also prevalent. Meat is used as a condiment, and oil is the predominant cooking fat. Often, several dishes are brought to the table and diners help themselves to small portions of each. Fried foods do appear on menus, but they are eaten in small amounts.

CHINESE RESTAURANTS

● ● ● ●

MANY SMART CHOICES

Y*ou can find many excellent dishes at a Chinese restaurant, but there are just as many dietary disasters.*

TIPS

● Some restaurants offer brown rice as an alternative to white or fried rice. Order it and you'll get double the fiber.

● Chinese food is usually low in artery-clogging trans fats because it's fried in oils that are liquid at room temperature, not hydrogenated oils that are solid at room temperature. Egg rolls are one popular exception.

Brown rice

Stir-frying is a common—and healthful—cooking method used throughout Asia.

WHAT'S IN IT?

Order something with vegetables in the name: Beef with Broccoli, Chicken with Asparagus, or Pork with Bok Choy ensure that you'll get some greens; dishes like Shrimp in Lobster Sauce, Pang Pang Chicken, and Pork in Black Bean Sauce don't.

WHAT'S THE BEST?

● Stir-fried dishes are among the most healthful you'll find on any menu at any restaurant. Full of fresh vegetables and quickly cooked in a small amount of oil, they retain most of their vitamins.

● Steamed dishes. Cooked over simmering water—not additional fat—these have a pure taste. Learn to appreciate the subtle flavors rather than mask them with salty or sweet condiments.

Eating with chopsticks takes practice, but it's an easy way to reduce calories, fat, and carbs.

SMART CHOICES

▼▼ Chopsticks. There are lots of benefits to using chopsticks rather than a fork. Each bite is limited by the amount you can grasp, rather than scoop; and because the bites are smaller, you eat more slowly; chopsticks also allow any starchy or oily sauces to drip off the food.

▼▼ Tofu. If you're leery of cooking it at home, try it in an Asian restaurant first. (Ask how it's prepared, though—sometimes it's deep-fried.) Because tofu is rather bland, try it in a restaurant that specializes in Hunan or Szechuan cooking. Dishes from these regions are highly seasoned; garlic, ginger, peppercorns, and hot chiles are common.

▼ Hot and sour. The heat comes from chiles or pepper, the sour from vinegar. Whether the term describes a meat or vegetable dish or, more commonly, soup, this means high flavor, but usually not high calories.

WHAT'S NOT SO GOOD?

● Floured and fried. General Tso's chicken, sweet-and-sour pork, and orange beef are just a few dishes where the meat is dipped in flour or batter and then fried till crispy. Steer clear of high-fat, high-carb meals.

● Sauces. Typically thickened with cornstarch, often sweetened, and almost always high in sodium, sauces can also be high in MSG (see page 95) and, depending on the dish, in fat. When you serve yourself, use a slotted spoon to leave most of the sauce in the container or bowl.

NOT-SO-SMART CHOICES

▲▲ Sweet-and-sour. At some restaurants, this means a lurid orange sauce; at most places, it's excessively high in refined carbs.

▲▲ Nuts. Although they are good for you, your favorite Chinese dish may have far more of them than the recommended ounce or so per day. If you order dishes with peanuts or anything with cashews, limit the number of nuts you eat to around 20 or so.

▲▲▲ Fried rice. Save on the calories, fat, and cholesterol (fried rice often includes egg), and eat your meal with brown or plain white rice.

CHINESE

● ● ● ●

MANY SMART CHOICES

There's a world of difference between Chinese takeout-type places and classical Chinese cuisine. If you find yourself in a fine Chinese restaurant, allow yourself to experience exquisitely prepared fresh seafood and vegetables.

● Mandarin, Mongolian, and Beijing- (or Peking-) style dishes usually contain meat and wheat; noodles and pancakes are common. Sauces tend to be heavy.

● If you ate Chinese food as a kid, you probably ate Cantonese-style dishes. Authentically, these dishes are heavy on vegetables and fish, with light sauces. Steaming, stir-frying, and roasting are common.

● Shanghai is renowned for its wonderful fish and vegetable dishes. Cooking from this region tends to use more oil than others; braised dishes, sometimes called red-cooked, are simmered in a sweetened soy sauce-based liquid.

● Western China's Szechuan and Hunan provinces are known for fiery foods.

WHAT'S IN IT?

Chinese cooking is so diverse that it's impossible to generalize about what the dishes contain—though it's a safe bet that most contain generous amounts of rice or noodles, depending on the region they come from.

Stir-fried vegetables make one of the healthiest options you can choose. The ingredients are heated quickly in a wok, retaining many of their nutrients.

Noodles

Cooked white rice

WHAT'S THE BEST?

● Steamed or stir-fried vegetables, or Buddha's Delight. With several different vegetables, these are among the lowest-fat, lowest-calorie, and most nutrient-rich dishes on a menu.

WHAT'S NOT SO GOOD?

● MSG (monosodium glutamate). If you're sensitive to the effects of this additive, look on the menu to be sure that the restaurant doesn't use MSG; don't simply rely on a waiter's promise that your dish won't include this flavor enhancer. It may in fact not be added to your order, but MSG is often used in stocks, sauces, and other components of Chinese dishes.

SMART CHOICES

▼▼ Keep an eye out for baked, broiled, steamed, stir-fried, and braised on menus; these are generally low-fat cooking methods.

▼ Steamed vegetable or shrimp dumplings. Tasty, filling, and virtually fat-free, these make a perfect light meal. If you don't think they're enough to satisfy you, order a bowl of soup, too.

NOT-SO-SMART CHOICES

▲▲▲ Barbecued spareribs. These are among the highest-fat cuts of pork; slather them with a sweet sauce and you'll end up with more than 100 calories per rib.

▲▲ Dry-fried and dry-cooked food. If these terms conjure images of pans devoid of oil, you've brought forth the wrong mental picture. These techniques involve deep-frying in very hot oil. The words sizzling, crispy, and creaky translate to "fried," too.

▲▲ Cold noodles with peanut sauce. Whether they go by this name or are called cold sesame noodles, these are high in calories, fat, and carbs. Pass them by.

NOODLE SHOPS AND DIM SUM PARLORS

● ●

SOME SMART CHOICES

There's little in a dim sum or noodle restaurant that qualifies as low-carb, but you'll find a fair number of low-fat options.

TIP

● It may not be readily discernible, but dishes at a dim sum restaurant are brought out in order: first come lightly steamed dishes, then exotic ones (such as chicken feet), then deep-fried foods, then desserts. Eat more at the beginning of the meal; less toward the end.

Colorful vegetables like sugar snap peas add flavor, crunch, and nutrition to noodle dishes.

WHAT'S IN IT?

Dim sum involves lots of different dishes. Food isn't prepared to order; instead, you select from carts that the waiters roll past. Most dishes are steamed or deep-fried.

WHAT'S THE BEST?

● Noodle dishes are often served in a broth with meat and vegetables. At some restaurants, you can build your own bowl, choosing the noodles (thin, flat, or fat), the type of broth, and any additions.

WHAT'S NOT SO GOOD?

● Resist the urge to pile your plate with lots of deep-fried dim sum. Egg rolls, spring rolls, won tons, pot stickers (fried dumplings), and fried buns are all high in carbohydrate as well as fat.

Noodles

SMART CHOICES

▼ Though the contents look like soup, noodle bowls are often eaten with chopsticks. You pick out the solids, then sip the broth. Portions are often huge, so don't feel that you must eat everything. Ask for a container to take some home in.

▼ Most noodle dishes use meat as a condiment, rather than as a "centerpiece." If you're looking to cut out saturated fat, these make ideal entrées.

▼ If you're watching your carb intake, look for soba on the menu. These Japanese noodles are made from buckwheat and have about one-third fewer carbs than wheat, rice, or bean noodles.

▼ Among the steamed dim sum dishes are pork spareribs—not the best choice—plus steamed buns stuffed with vegetables or pork, and shrimp dumplings. If you're feeling adventurous, try steamed chicken feet.

NOT-SO-SMART CHOICES

▲▲ Though ramen noodles have a texture similar to spaghetti, they're not air-dried. Instead, they're "dried" by deep-frying and are best avoided.

▲▲ Gow gee (fried won tons stuffed with shrimp and vegetables), pearl balls (sticky rice wrapped around ground pork), wu gok (a turnover made with taro, a very starchy vegetable), and siu mai (another fried won ton dish) are all high in carbohydrate and fat.

▲ Skipping tea. Dim sum evolved from the snacks served at tea houses; because tea aids digestion, somewhat dense fried foods were tolerable to their patrons. Keep refilling your cup to avoid any feelings of heaviness.

Noodles come in a range of guises, from cellophane and ramen noodles to egg and rice noodles, and ranging in size from thin to fat.

JAPANESE

● ● ● ●

MANY SMART CHOICES

Japan's cuisine reflects the country's geography: seafood dishes abound, and beef, which is very expensive to raise, makes less-frequent appearances on menus.

Steak teriyaki made with whole-wheat noodles and beef tenderloin contains protein and vitamin B12, although this is offset by the sugar in the marinade.

Tofu

WHAT'S IN IT?

In addition to seafood, vegetables, tofu, and noodle dishes, one-pot meals such as *shabu-shabu* are common on Japanese menus.

WHAT'S THE BEST?

● Miso soup. A blend of miso paste (from soybeans), *kombu* (a type of seaweed), and *dashi* (a broth made of dried bonito flakes), this flavorful soup makes a perfect beginning to a meal.

● Green tea. Made from unfermented tea leaves, green tea is almost free of caffeine and very high in potent antioxidants called polyphenols. Sip it throughout your meal—and leave the sugar out.

WHAT'S NOT SO GOOD?

● *Tempura*. Most commonly vegetables or shrimp dipped in a batter and then deep-fried, *tempura* is no lighter than any other cuisine's battered and fried dishes. The dipping sauces that accompany it are often high in sodium or sugar.

SMART CHOICES

▼▲ Vegetables. Japanese cuisine uses vegetables like lotus root, daikon, burdock, and Japanese eggplant. If you've seen them in supermarkets but haven't cooked with them, try them in a Japanese restaurant to see how you like them prepared, then make them at home.

▼▼ *Shabu-shabu*. This dish enables diners to dip vegetables and meats into a simmering broth (not into fat, as with cheese fondue).

▼▼ Condiments. Japanese flavorings include dried bonito (a type of fish), *ponzu* (a dipping sauce made of soy sauce, rice-wine vinegar, *dashi*, and seaweed), *wasabi* (pungent horseradish paste), pickled ginger, *shoyu* (Japanese soy sauce), and *mirin* (rice wine). All are low-fat, low-carb ways to add big flavor.

NOT-SO-SMART CHOICES

▲▲▲ Fried vegetable dumplings. Called *gyoza*, these are sometimes referred to as "pot stickers." Order grilled eggplant or other vegetables instead.

▲ Yakitori. If you're watching your carbs, beware of these skewers of chicken strips; the meat is marinated in a sweet soy-based sauce. Try *negimaki*—thin slices of beef wrapped around scallions, then grilled—instead.

Kombu

Nori

SUSHI AND SASHIMI

• • • •

MANY SMART CHOICES

*C*ontrary to popular belief, sushi refers to anything made with vinegared rice; it may include vegetables and cooked or raw foods; sashimi refers to raw fish.

WHAT'S IN IT?

Sushi includes seafood and shellfish, but may also feature vegetables; most often the seafood is raw, but it may be cooked. It's typically served with vinegared rice and may be rolled within sheets of seaweed, called *nori*.

Sushi wrapped in sheets of nori *make appealing canapés or picnic foods and are served cold.*

WHAT'S THE BEST?

● Seaweed. Whether it's *kombu* (sometimes spelled *konbu*), which is a type of kelp, or *nori*, which is made from purple laver, sea greens are incredibly high in protein, iron, calcium, and vitamins.

TIP

● Most sushi and sashimi restaurants fly in fish every day. Some restaurants have tanks with live fish in them, and the fish are prepared when ordered.

SMART CHOICES

▼ *Yaki.* This term means grilled or broiled; these foods will generally be low in fat.

▲ *Ji-.* This prefix indicates locally caught or locally produced foods.

▼▼ *Maki.* This means rolled; usually it refers to foods wrapped in sheets of seaweed, but California rolls have rice on the outside. *Tekka-maki* is tuna; *kappa-maki* is cucumber roll.

▼▲ Tuna. This goes by a number of names, based on the fish's age, what part of the body it is cut from, and the species. *Tekka* generally indicates tuna in a roll. *Toro, marguro, ahi,* and *ahimi* all mean tuna; *otoro* is the fattiest tuna cut from the lower belly; *chutoro* is moderately fatty. *Hamachi* is yellowtail, a tunalike fish; *inada* and *kanbachi* are very young yellowtail.

WHAT'S NOT SO GOOD?

● Anything less than pristine conditions. Any fish that is eaten raw should be impeccably fresh, the food-preparation area should be spotless, and the fish should be properly stored and handled. Any compromises can result in disease.

NOT-SO-SMART CHOICES

▲▲ *Agemono.* Foods cooked this way are either pan-fried or deep-fried; *tempura* is the most common example, but you may find others on Japanese menus.

▼ *Oshinko.* These pickled vegetables (usually cucumbers) are salt-cured; eat them in moderation if you are sensitive to too much sodium.

Nori salad, made by roasting sheets of nori *until crisp, then mixing it with vegetables, is high in magnesium.*

THAI

MANY SMART CHOICES

Intriguing flavors, harmoniously blended, make Thai cuisine one of the most universally popular.

TIP

● If you see *pad* on a menu, you know the dish will include noodles. *Pad thai* is a classic; this popular dish includes rice noodles, tofu, shrimp, peanuts, garlic, chiles, nam pla, bean sprouts, and eggs.

WHAT'S IN IT?

Most Thai dishes combine four flavor elements: hot, sour, salty, and sweet. A variety of seasonings—ranging from limes and herbs (like lemongrass and basil) to *nam pla* (a thin, salty sauce made from fermented fish) and very hot chiles—add pizzazz.

WHAT'S THE BEST?

● Salads. Unlike greens-based salads, Thai salads (called *yam* or *yum*) are made with vegetables and noodles. Meat salads, called *larb*, are dressed in a sauce made of *nam pla*, chiles, garlic, and lime juice. Watch for the dressings, though—they may include peanuts.

Lemongrass is a ubiquitous Thai ingredient that has now found widespread use in the West.

Spring rolls

WHAT'S NOT SO GOOD?

● Portion sizes. Because Thai dishes are meant to be served family-style, you'll often be brought a large serving of whatever it is that you order.

● Bird chiles. These tiny chiles are named for their resemblance to a bird's beak. They can be red or green, but they are quite fiery. Take care that you don't bite into one unexpectedly.

SMART CHOICES

▲ Family-style. Most Thai restaurants accommodate the Western preference for individual entrées, but in Thailand most meals are served family-style—a variety of dishes are placed on the table and diners help themselves. A typical meal includes a hot curry, cold salad, vegetable, and a soup.

▼▲ Soups. *Tom yum koong* and *tom yum kai* are savory soups in a hot-and-sour broth. The former includes shrimp and mushrooms; the latter, vegetables.

▼ Steamed dumplings. These are often in wrappers that are so delicate they're virtually translucent.

▼▼▲ Seafood. Authentic Thai cuisine boasts plenty of fish dishes. Try steamed mussels in a garlic-and-herb broth, sautéed scallops with basil and chiles, or fishcakes.

NOT-SO-SMART CHOICES

▲ Curries. Meat and vegetables simmered in a broth of coconut milk and curry paste, curries come in varying heat levels. Green is the hottest, red is moderately hot, and yellow is the mildest. It's difficult to tell how much fat such dishes may contain, so eat them in small amounts.

▲▲ Spring rolls. Although these are smaller than egg rolls, they're still deep-fried.

▲▲ Satay. If the menu doesn't say, ask the server what is in the marinade. Sometimes these skewered foods can be marinated in sweetened sauces; satay is usually served with a high-fat peanut sauce.

▲ Deep-fried whole fish with a sweet-and-sour sauce belies the reputation of Thai food as healthful.

VIETNAMESE

● ● ● ●

MANY SMART CHOICES

*V*ietnam's cuisine is similar to China's and Thailand's; however, you may find French influences on the menu as well.

TIP

● Vietnamese food is meant to be served family-style. To experience a wide variety of flavors, textures, and cooking methods, order a steamed dish, a fried dish, a simmered dish, a rice or noodle dish, and a roast to share among several diners.

Rice papers are traditionally used in Vietnam to encase a filling of vegetables, seafood, or meats.

WHAT'S IN IT?

Ginger, lime, lemongrass, tamarind, mint, and peanut are the dominant flavorings; garlic and *nuoc mam* (sometimes called *nuoc cham*, the Vietnamese version of fish sauce) are prevalent as well.

WHAT'S THE BEST?

● Spring rolls are deep-fried, but salad rolls (sometimes called summer rolls) are made of rice-paper sheets that are soaked until pliable, then wrapped around fillings of finely chopped vegetables, meats, seafood, or a combination of these.

Peanuts

SMART CHOICES

▼ Vietnamese cuisine tends to be light in texture, with delicate flavors. Most dishes are fairly low in fat.

▲ *Canh chua.* This hot-and-sour soup features pineapple, tomato, celery, mushrooms, and herbs, and can often include fish, chicken, vegetables, or won tons. It is sometimes called Vietnamese bouillabaisse.

▼ *La sa* and *pho. La sa* is a curry-infused soup made with coconut milk; *pho* is a broth. Both contain generous amounts of vegetables, but they also include noodles, and are not the best choices if you are controlling your carbohydrates.

NOT-SO-SMART CHOICES

▲ Caramel sauce. If you see *nuoc duong thang* on menus, you know you'll get a high-sodium, high-sugar sauce (it's made by combining *nuoc mam* with melted sugar). It's often used in simmered dishes.

▲▲ Barbecued spareribs. If you want a nibble with which to start your meal, order grilled vegetables on skewers instead.

▲ *Xao gung.* You might see *thit xao gung, tom xao gung,* or *ga xao gung*—this is pork, shrimp, or chicken in a honey sauce. It's higher in carbohydrate than many dishes.

The distinctive flavors of Vietnamese cooking include tamarind, ginger, garlic, and lime, which add sourness, heat, and pungency to a variety of dishes.

WHAT'S NOT SO GOOD?

● Peanuts. They appear in several Vietnamese salads and many sauces. Although they add flavor and crunch, they also impart plenty of fat and calories. If your appetizer includes them, order an entrée that doesn't.

KOREAN

SOME SMART CHOICES

*K**orean cuisine is similar to Japanese and Chinese cooking, with some differences. It uses more beef and less seafood than Japanese cooking, and less oil than Chinese, and it tends to be spicier than both.*

White long-grain rice

TIP

● Rice, called *bap*, and rice noodles, known as *chapchae*, form the base of most dishes. *Duboo*, or bean curd, is also common.

Chow-mein-style dishes such as chapchae *are made of noodles stir-fried with vegetables such as mushrooms, bean sprouts, cucumber, zucchini, and scallions.*

WHAT'S IN IT?

Korean cuisine is light on fresh vegetables. The cold climate and short growing season mean that, historically, most vegetables were preserved, usually by pickling. *Kimchi* is the Korean word for vegetables; it also refers to the ubiquitous dish of pickled vegetables.

WHAT'S THE BEST?

● Like Thai and Chinese meals, Korean meals are often served family-style. By taking small amounts of different dishes, you can experience a wide variety of flavors and textures without overeating.

WHAT'S NOT SO GOOD?

● Few fresh vegetables. If you're going to a Korean restaurant for a dinner, have a vegetable-based soup or salad (or both) at lunch, and snack on fresh fruit.

Turnip, cucumber, and cabbage are common ingredients of the pickled vegetable dish known as kimchi.

Cucumber

Turnip

SMART CHOICES

▼ Beef appears in a variety of guises. *Bulgogi*, or barbecue; *mandoo guk*, a beef stew served with dumplings and *galbi tang*, a stew made of beef ribs, are common.

▼ *Kimchi* appears at every meal, every day; this dish of pickled vegetables can include any vegetables, but the most common are cabbages, turnips, and cucumbers in a brine of chiles, garlic, onions, ginger, fish sauce, oyster sauce, and salt.

▲ *Panchan*. As many as 20 different side dishes and condiments form part of an authentic Korean meal. These are used to balance the meal's flavors and textures.

Cabbage

NOT-SO-SMART CHOICES

▲ *Bimibap*, a casserole made of rice with meat, vegetables, and egg, is high in refined carbohydrate.

▲ *Chapchae*, a dish of stir-fried noodles, is similar to China's chow mein.

▲ *Jogae pa jon*, a rice and scallion pancake, can be extremely high in sodium.

INDIAN

● ● ● ●

MANY SMART CHOICES

India's cooking shares certain elements of its flavors, its techniques, and its ingredients with other Asian countries.

WHAT'S IN IT?

Indian cuisine may include lamb and poultry, but pork appears only rarely on the menu, and beef is almost never an option. You will also find an incredible array of vegetarian dishes from which to choose.

WHAT'S THE BEST?

● *Raita.* A refreshingly cool sauce made of yogurt and cucumbers, this is a must in order to tame the heat of spicy dishes like *vindaloo*.

WHAT'S NOT SO GOOD?

● Chutneys. These sour-sweet, fruit-based condiments are high in carbohydrate. Use them in moderation if you're limiting your refined carbs.

● Ghee. One of the common cooking fats in India, *ghee* is butter with the milk solids removed. It's somewhat higher in cholesterol and saturated fat than butter is.

ABOVE Pakora *with mint and tomato chutney is an appetizing dish, but is high in fat and carbs.*

LEFT *Phyllo pastry packages stuffed with a range of ingredients, samosas make a delicious snack or vegetarian option.*

SMART CHOICES

▼ *Lassi.* A shake made of yogurt, *lassi* can be either sweet or savory, depending on whether it is made with fruit or herbs.

▼▼ *Paneer.* A fresh cheese, this appears on menus as *saag paneer* (cooked with spinach and spices) or *shahi paneer* (cooked in a tomato sauce).

▼▼ *Tandoori.* A *tandoor* is a cylindrical clay oven in which meats and breads are cooked. Meats are typically coated with a spicy blend of seasonings and skewered before cooking. The seasonings impart a bright reddish-orange color, so the name *tandoori* has come to refer to any foods with these spices, and not just those cooked in a *tandoor*.

NOT-SO-SMART CHOICES

▲▲▲ *Samosas.* These triangular pastries can be stuffed with vegetables, meat, or both; they're usually fried. In India they're sold from pushcarts, and appear on menus as appetizers.

▲▲ *Pakora.* Small fritters made of chickpea flour, these deep-fried appetizers can include vegetables, fruit, rice, meat, or fish.

▲ *Korma.* If you're watching your fat intake, look out for *korma.* This is cubed meat cooked in a creamy curry sauce.

INDIAN

● ● ● ●

MANY SMART CHOICES

"*Indian food" makes about as much sense as "European food"—this country's diverse culture and climate combine to make it diverse culinarily, too.*

WHAT'S IN IT?

Although beef seldom, if ever, appears on Indian menus, dairy food—yogurt, buttermilk, fresh cheeses, cream, and sour cream—is a common ingredient in many dishes.

TIP

● It isn't uncommon for baskets of *chapati*, *roti*, *naan*, and *paratha* to appear on tables. Use the same discretion with these as you do with bread-and-butter or garlic-bread baskets.

WHAT'S THE BEST?

● *Tikka*, like kabobs, are skewers of meat and vegetables. They may be marinated before cooking.

● Family-style. By ordering several dishes to share among your table, you can get a variety of flavors and textures—and nutrients.

WHAT'S NOT SO GOOD?

● Buffets. Although these give you the opportunity to enjoy a variety of foods, it's all too easy to eat too much when you go down a buffet line. Foods tend to be less fresh, too.

Yogurt

Buttermilk

Chickpeas are packed with protein, vitamins A, B-complex, and C, and minerals.

Curried cauliflower is one of numerous Indian vegetarian dishes.

SMART CHOICES

▼▼ Vegetarian and vegetable dishes. Whether you opt to start with a vegetable appetizer or choose cauliflower curry as an entrée—or both—Indian menus abound with an almost overwhelming assortment of vegetable dishes.

▼ *Dal.* Whether it's spelled *dal*, *dhal*, or *dhall*, this refers to legumes like lentils, peas, and beans. Sometimes they're ground into flours for use in breads; they're also used whole in a variety of vegetable dishes.

NOT-SO-SMART CHOICES

▲ *Vindaloo.* Depending on their ingredients, *vindaloos* can be high in fat. These curries are also incredibly fiery. If you're not familiar with their heat, proceed cautiously. Have a yogurt-based side dish or drink to help cool your mouth.

▲▲ *Biryani.* A northern Indian dish where rice, meats, dried fruits, and nuts are seasoned and baked, *biryani* can be high in both fat and carbohydrate.

▲ Oil. Breads like *poori* and most eggplant dishes can be extremely high in fat.

EUROPEAN
RESTAURANTS

EUROPEAN RESTAURANTS

Thanks to travel and television, ingredients and dishes that were once local or regional specialties can now be found around the world. Northern Italy's risotto appears on menus from Dublin to Denver, and cravings for fish and chips can be met from San Diego to Singapore—and not just in Italian or English restaurants. You might find Chicken Francese—a dish in the French style, with the Italian spelling—on a menu in an Irish pub in the United States.

In fact, there is considerable overlap between dishes and countries. Borders shift, but crops don't change, and it can be difficult (if not impossible) to determine the actual provenance of a dish. In other cases, nationality counts for less than proximity: northern Italy's cuisine probably has more in common with Austria's, France's, and Switzerland's than it does with the cooking of southern Italy and Sicily.

ENGLISH

● ●

SOME SMART CHOICES

Often derided for its bland food, England is actually home to some amazingly flavorful condiments and sauces.

Beef pot roast

A pot roast or pot pie makes a hearty, warming dish for a cold day, and good use of a variety of root vegetables.

TIP

● Traditionally, shepherd's pie is made with lamb; cottage pie is made with beef. Both dishes are topped with a mashed potato crust. Pot pies are covered with puff pastry or pie crust.

The term "shepherd's pie" reflects its content of ground lamb, with a soft potato topping.

WHAT'S IN IT?

Because England's climate is comparatively harsh, its cuisine relies more heavily on root vegetables and hardy greens than on the more tender bell peppers, tomatoes, and similar vegetables that thrive further south in Europe near the Mediterranean.

Venison slices

Cod with winter vegetables

WHAT'S THE BEST?

● Fish and shellfish appear in many guises, ranging from basic cod dishes to more exotic langoustines. Avoid dishes that are battered or breaded, and deep-fried or sauced with cream.

WHAT'S NOT SO GOOD?

● Sausages. Whether combined with potatoes in the traditional "bangers and mash," layered in batter in "toad-in-the-hole," or wrapped around a hard-cooked egg in Scotch eggs, sausages are high in fat.

SMART CHOICES

▼▼ Game. You're likely to find venison and pheasant on menus. Even when it's farm raised, most game animals yield meat that is far leaner than that of domestic animals. As a bonus, these meats are often simply prepared—as a roast, for example—and served with a sauce on the side.

▼ Sauces and condiments. From tangy Cumberland sauce to pungent Worcestershire and sharp mustards, condiments add flair to foods that might otherwise seem bland.

▼ Tea. Small sandwiches have built-in portion control. Just take care you don't go overboard on the scones with clotted cream and jam.

NOT-SO-SMART CHOICES

▲▲ Ploughman's lunch. If you're lucky, you might find this on a menu with an outstanding farmhouse cheese. If not, save your calories and fat grams for something else.

▲▲▲ Fish and chips. Any nutritional benefits to be gained from the potatoes or the fish are long gone by the time these emerge from the deep fryer.

▲▲▲ Welsh rarebit. Lots of cheese melted over a thick slice of toasted country white bread and topped with tomatoes. Comforting? Yes. Healthful? Not exactly.

SPANISH

● ● ● ●

MANY SMART CHOICES

*S*panish cuisine features plenty
of seafood and vegetables.
You'll also find terrific hams
on many menus.

Olives

Sardines

WHAT'S IN IT?

The predominant cooking fat in Spain
is olive oil; butter is used in desserts,
but rarely for sautéing. Garlic, smoked
paprika, and peppers (especially
piquillo) season many dishes.

BELOW *Tapas refers to the range of
small dishes served with drinks in
most Spanish bars and restaurants.*

Opt for tortillas that contain vegetables rather than high-fat ingredients such as chorizo.

WHAT'S THE BEST?

● If you're not familiar with Spanish foods and flavors, order tapas. These can be as simple as marinated olives and cheese, or more complicated dishes like shrimp in garlic and the tiny turnovers called *empanadillas*.

WHAT'S NOT SO GOOD?

● Tortillas. Unlike the Mexican flatbread, a Spanish tortilla is an open-face egg dish, similar to a *frittata*. It's often cut into wedges and served at room temperature.

SMART CHOICES

▼▼▼ Seafood. Squid, shrimp, and octopus, as well as fish like sardines, mackerel, anchovies, and *bacalao* (dried and salted cod), are common on Spanish menus. Sardines and mackerel are among the highest foods in heart-healthy omega-3s.

▼ *Jamon serrano.* Similar (though some people think far superior) to Italy's *prosciutto di Parma*, Spain's fabled ham is often served thinly sliced and in small portions.

▼▲ Soups. *Caldo gallego, gazpacho,* and garlic soup are all high in vegetables and broth-based. They're an ideal appetizer or light meal.

NOT-SO-SMART CHOICES

▲▲▲ Watch out for the words *empanados* and *estofadalo* on Spanish menus. The first term indicates that the food is breaded (and usually fried); the second term means smothered (or it can mean stew).

▲ *Chorizo.* A thin, highly spiced sausage, *chorizo* is fine as part of a tapas plate, or as flavoring in a dish, but it's quite high in fat and is best avoided as an entrée.

▲▲▲ Paella. *Valenciana* indicates sausage and chicken; *marinera* or *mariscos* signify seafood only. This labor-intensive dish is often available only in portions suitable for two or more diners.

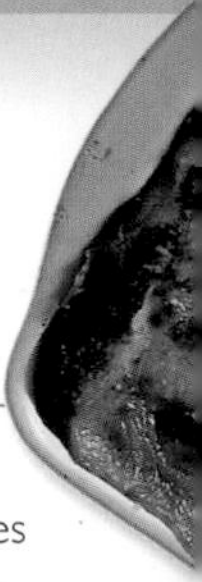

ITALIAN

● ● ● ●

MANY SMART CHOICES

*A*uthentic Italian food can be among the most nutritious and most flavorful that you're likely to find in southern Europe.

Zucchini

Veal

WHAT'S IN IT?

Italian food traditionally features plenty of vegetables, from artichokes to zucchini. Fish and chicken appear on menus far more often than beef or pork. Cheese appears in smaller amounts than it does in many American interpretations.

WHAT'S THE BEST?

● *Alla Fiorentina* means "in the style of Florence"; when these words describe a dish, it means that spinach will be an ingredient.

● *Al forno*, or "from the oven," is another good term to look for. Roasts and baked dishes—so long as they are not smothered with cheese—are generally low in fat.

T I P

● *Primavera* means "spring green," and while a *primavera* sauce typically includes vegetables, such dishes can vary according to the season. However, *primavera* sauce may include cream, too; if the menu doesn't say, make sure that you ask.

Lasagna

Lasagna and focaccia: the former is more of an American-Italian invention; the latter, the real thing.

WHAT'S NOT SO GOOD?

● Bruschetta. Often brushed with oil before and during grilling, this bread can be surprisingly high in fat. Focaccia is brushed with olive oil before baking and it, too, can contain more fat than you might at first suspect.

SMART CHOICES

▼▼ *Pancetta.* This Italian bacon is just as fatty as American bacon, but it's typically used in very small amounts as a flavoring, rather than as a dish unto itself.

▼▼ Veal. Cheese-smothered veal *parmigiana* isn't a smart choice, but *vitello tonnato* (veal with tuna sauce), veal *piccata*, and veal Marsala are generally good choices.

NOT-SO-SMART CHOICES

▲▲ Antipasto platters. Heavy on the meat and cheese, and light on the vegetables, these are best split between several diners rather than eaten individually.

▲▲ *Panini.* These "little sandwiches" are often pressed (and if so, they aren't so bad). However, some *panini* are grilled or made with high-fat breads like focaccia. As with all sandwiches, watch the fillings.

▲▲▲ Lasagna. More of an Italian-American dish than an authentically Italian one, this cheesy, meaty baked pasta is heavy and is high in calories, fat, and carbs.

▲▲ *Alla Vodka.* If you've never heard this called "vodka cream sauce," you may be surprised to learn that this sauce does contain cream—often considerable amounts.

ITALIAN

MANY SMART CHOICES

Food from the south of Italy tends to be more robust in style; northern Italian food is by no means bland, but it tends to be more delicate in flavor.

TIP

● Cheese ravioli, *manicotti*, lasagna, and stuffed shells contain ricotta, a fresh cheese that helps to make these dishes a very rich source of calcium. However, the cheese is often the full-fat variety, and fresh cheeses also tend to be high in carbohydrate.

WHAT'S IN IT?

Fish, including pungent anchovies, makes frequent appearances in Italian dishes. Don't shy away from menu offerings that include them—anchovies often provide a wonderful depth of flavor, and they are high in omega-3 fats.

WHAT'S THE BEST?

● Polenta. Made of cornmeal, this peasant dish from the Piedmont region is lower in carbohydrate than pasta, bread, or rice.

WHAT'S NOT SO GOOD?

● Pesto. Just because it's green doesn't mean it's low-calorie. Thanks to lots of olive oil and plenty of pine nuts, this green paste can have as many as 300 calories in a ¼-cup … and restaurants often use two or three times that amount on a serving of pasta.

● Exploding portions. Pasta is inexpensive, and it isn't uncommon for restaurants to serve up 4-cup portions. Consider that a box of pasta gives a serving size as ½ cup cooked, however.

Tagliatelle is just one of Italy's numerous pasta variations.

Ricotta

It's the slow cooking of arborio rice in a traditional Italian risotto that helps to impart flavor and creaminess.

SMART CHOICES

▼▼▼ Vegetables. Artichokes, tomatoes, bell peppers, and broccoli rabe are just some of the vegetables that flourish in Italy's mild Mediterranean climate and are featured in many recipes. You might even see *cavalo nero*, or black cabbage, on menus.

▼▼▲ Soups. Most Italian soups are broth- or vegetable-based; few are cream-based. (*Zuppa* refers to a thick soup often served over bread; *minestra* to a thinner soup that includes vegetables or pieces of meat; *brodo* means broth.) Order one of these to begin your meal.

NOT-SO-SMART CHOICES

▲▲ Risotto. High in refined carbohydrate and often high in fat, this dish can include saffron and marrow (the classic *risotto Milanese*), seafood or meat, vegetables, or simply Parmesan.

▲ Butter. Although olive oil is the predominant cooking fat in southern Italy, butter is commonly used in the north.

▲▲ Garlic bread. Half a loaf, slathered with butter and chopped garlic, adds up to a fabulous number of calories, fat, saturated fat, and refined carbohydrate. If you must order garlic bread, split it among several diners.

▲▲ Fritto misto. Translating literally as "fried mix," this is a plate of battered and deep-fried vegetables, meat, eggs, and seafood.

▲ Sausage and pepperoni. Meat makes infrequent appearances on Italian tables—it's expensive, and seafood is considerably more plentiful. This very fatty meat is acceptable in small amounts—say, topping a pizza—but it's best to avoid it as the focal point of a dish.

ITALIAN

● ● ● ●

MANY SMART CHOICES

Shrimp

It's almost impossible to imagine Italian food without tomatoes, although they were not used widely until the late 1800s.

Tomato paste

Tomato

Eggplant

WHAT'S IN IT?

Cooked tomatoes are incredibly high in lycopene, a carotenoid pigment that has powerful antioxidant properties and which may help to prevent against some forms of cancer. Tomatoes are high in vitamin C, too, as well as being low in sodium and high in potassium.

WHAT'S THE BEST?

● Pungent, high-flavor sauces like *arrabbiata*, *puttanesca*, and *fra diavolo* often taste better without the ubiquitous Parmesan cheese that we tend to sprinkle all over them; this enables you to savor their true taste.

WHAT'S NOT SO GOOD?

● Bread. Whether it comes with butter or adorable little plates and a bottle of olive oil, pass on the pre-dinner bread whenever possible, especially if you're ordering pasta as an entrée. It simply increases your carb and fat intake.

TIP

● Shellfish appears frequently on Italian menus. Pass on the deep-fried *calamari* and Clams Casino, and if the scampi is swimming in oil, hold the shrimp out of the oil so that some can drip off before eating.

NOT-SO-SMART CHOICES

▲▲ Spaghetti with meatballs. This entrée often comes with two or three meatballs and may contain more than a ¼ pound of ground beef.

▲▲ Eggplant *parmigiana*. Breaded and fried, then covered with a thick blanket of mozzarella, this vegetable dish is even higher in calories and fat than veal or chicken *parmigiana*. Eggplant acts like a sponge and absorbs far more oil than most other foods do.

▲▲ *Carbonara*. Made with egg yolks, heavy cream, and plenty of Parmesan cheese, this is a very rich sauce and has the calories to match.

Alfredo. Made of heavy cream, butter, and cheese, this sauce contains excessively high calories, total fat, and saturated fat. Whether it's tossed with fettuccine, spooned over chicken, or adapted to make a salad dressing, this is one sauce to avoid at all costs.

SMART CHOICES

▽▲ *Marinara.* A highly seasoned sauce of tomatoes, onions, garlic, and oregano, *marinara* is an excellent choice whether you're eating low-fat or low-carb. It's most commonly used to sauce pasta, but is also used on pizzas and with meats.

▽▽ Meat sauce. Leaner than meatballs or sausage, meat sauce includes enough meat to be satisfyingly hearty, but not so much as to derail you.

▽▽ Clam sauce. Garlicky and broth-based, this flavorsome sauce usually goes with spaghetti or linguine.

Parmesan

Carbonara

FRENCH

● ●

SOME SMART CHOICES

Traditional French food has a reputation for being rich and heavy, though many restaurants serve much lighter fare than in past decades.

RIGHT *Vegetables roasted with olive oil and garlic are a feature of Provençal cooking.*

TIP

● Nouvelle cuisine is remembered most for its highly stylized arrangements of minuscule portions, but it also had a profound effect on how sauces were made: rather than being thickened with flour, they were reduced through boiling so that their flavors became much more concentrated.

WHAT'S IN IT?

Gone are the days when French food was covered in rich cream sauces—you'll be hard-pressed to find béarnaise, bordelaise, hollandaise, or parisienne sauces on menus today.

WHAT'S THE BEST?

● Provençal cooking is readily identifiable by its use of garlic, tomatoes, olives, and olive oil. Its robust flavors are inherently satisfying.

● Foods cooked *à la meunière* can be healthful. This term indicates that a food—often fish fillets or chicken—is dusted with flour and sautéed in butter. If done properly, a crust is formed and little fat is absorbed.

SMART CHOICES

▼▲ Cheese as dessert. Yes, cheese is high in fat and calories, but often considerably less than profiteroles or *tarte Tatin*. Research also suggests that some cheeses can help prevent tooth decay.

▼▼ *Salade Niçoise*. Often made without greens, this elegant salad usually features tomatoes, olives, green beans, potatoes, hard-cooked eggs, and tuna.

NOT-SO-SMART CHOICES

▲▲ *Bisque*. Thick and rich and full of cream, *bisque* is not the soup to order if you're watching your fat intake. Some restaurants call any thick puréed soup a *bisque*, whether it is thickened with cream or puréed vegetables.

▲ *Foie gras*. Literally "fat liver," *foie gras* can be prepared in a variety of ways, but none of them masks the fact that this is almost pure fat (it supplies a small amount of protein).

▲▲▲ *En croute*. Anything wrapped "in a crust" of pastry adds greatly to its fat and calorie counts.

▲▲▲ *Coquilles* St. Jacques. Scallops are one of the leanest sources of protein, but skip this dish if that's what you're hoping for. It features scallops in cream sauce, topped with bread crumbs and cheese, then broiled.

A tarte Tatin *is cooked, then turned upside down onto a plate so that the fruit (which might be apples, bananas, or pineapple) is on top.*

WHAT'S NOT SO GOOD?

● *Quenelles* are little dumplings. They may include meat or vegetables, but they are bound together with bread crumbs or flour, butter, and egg yolks. When they're served as a garnish or floated in a soup they are acceptable, but try to avoid them as an entrée.

● Served as an appetizer, *rillettes* consists of meat cooked in seasoned fat, and then pounded into a paste. It's packed into ramekins and chilled, then served as a spread.

125

FRENCH
● ●

SOME SMART CHOICES

French food can form part of a healthful diet—and not only when eaten with a glass of red wine. Keep portions small, just as they do in France.

Gruyère

Mussels

WHAT'S IN IT?

Gratins and *gratinées* aren't always full of cheese. Although *soupe à l'oignon gratinée* is covered with cheese (usually Swiss or Gruyère) before broiling, *gratin dauphinois* may or may not include it—though it does contain considerable cream and butter.

WHAT'S THE BEST?

● Stews. Take care to choose wine- or tomato-based stews, such as *bourguignonne* or Marengo, rather than *blanquettes*. They tend to contain less added fat and are full of rich, deep flavors.

WHAT'S NOT SO GOOD?

● Keep an eye out for *farce*, *farci*, and *farcis* on menus. *Farce* is the French word for stuffing—usually bread or bread crumbs, held together with plenty of fat.

● *Cordon bleu* starts with slices of Swiss cheese and ham wrapped in chicken-breast cutlets. The cutlets are then breaded and sautéed—hardly worthy of a nutritional blue ribbon.

Mushroom quiche

SMART CHOICES

▼▼ *Bouillabaisse.* This hearty stew is often served with red-pepper *rouille* on bread rounds. Skip these if you're watching your carbs.

▲ *Cassoulet.* The ingredients in this hearty bean dish can vary—different regions include different meats or sausages—but it is traditionally made with *confit*—duck legs cooked and preserved in duck fat. Sounds bad? Not really: It's actually lower in saturated fat than butter is.

▼ *Navarin.* Often made with lamb and vegetables such as peas, potatoes, turnips, onions, and beans, *navarin* tends to be one of the more delicately flavored stews.

Bouillabaise is a substantial fish stew.

NOT-SO-SMART CHOICES

▲▲ Quiche Lorraine. An authentic quiche Lorraine is made of eggs, cream, bacon, and seasonings baked in a tart crust; most versions now include cheese and onions.

▲▲ *Frites.* The French word for "fried," this can refer to any fried food, but it most frequently refers to French fries, sometimes called *pommes frites.*

▲ *Choucroute garni.* An Alsatian dish of smoked pork loin, veal sausage, pork breast, potatoes, and sauerkraut cooked in a white wine such as Pinot d'Alsace, this dish contains meats that are very high in fat.

▲▲ *Blanquette.* A stew finished with egg yolk and heavy cream, this pale stew (its name comes from the French word for white) is very rich.

127

GERMAN AND AUSTRIAN

● ●

SOME SMART CHOICES

Traditionally hearty fare, food from Germany and Austria tends to be heavy on sausages, meat with gravy, and root vegetables.

WHAT'S IN IT?

If you're a herring lover, be careful when ordering pickled herring. Sometimes it's simply herring in a spiced vinegar, but it can be pickled and then bottled in a sour-cream sauce. Rollmops are herring that are stuffed with pickle or onion before being preserved in spiced vinegar.

WHAT'S THE BEST?

● Red cabbage. Although it's often sweetened, red cabbage is high in a tremendous array of nutrients. It's an excellent source of anthocyanins, the plant pigments that make blueberries so healthful. Cabbage may also be cancer-protective.

TIP

● Order light at a German restaurant. It isn't unusual for potato salad and coleslaw to be brought to the table, as well as bread and butter. Frequently, meals come with soup and a salad as well.

Oven-baked red cabbage is an excellent accompaniment to fish or lean meat and contains vitamin C.

WHAT'S NOT SO GOOD?

● Most side dishes. Potato pancakes, *spaetzle*, potato salads, potato dumplings, *nockerl* (savory Austrian dumplings), and *schultzkrapfen* (Austrian cheese ravioli) are all heavy and starchy.

potato salad

SMART CHOICES

▼ Roasts. You may find roast game such as venison, fowl such as duck, or pork loin on menus. Typically cooked with little added fat (but often marinated in, or served with, a sweet-sour sauce), roasts make a good alternative to breaded entrées or fatty sausages.

▼ *Bauernschinken*. A smoked ham, this tends to be fairly lean.

Rösti usually refers to potatoes, but can also apply to vegetables.

NOT-SO-SMART CHOICES

▲▲ *Schnitzel*. A cutlet dipped in egg, then flour, then fried. *Wienerschnitzel* is made with veal; *jägerschnitzel* is a pork cutlet served in a mushroom wine gravy; and *schnitzel Holstein* is served with eggs and vegetables.

▲▼ *Wurst*. Whether made of veal (*weisswurst*), beef (*knockwurst*), liver (*leberwurst*), pork (*bratwurst*), or a combination thereof, most sausages are high in fats. The better ones are made of seasoned meats and don't contain starchy fillers.

▲▲ *Palatschinken*. Crêpes stacked six or eight high, layered with a savory filling of chopped fish, ham, veal, mushrooms, or other vegetables, then held together with sour cream or cream.

▲▲▲ *Strudel*. Most commonly associated with apples, *strudels* can be filled with savory mixtures as well. No matter how lean or low in carbohydrate the fillings are, the buttery-rich pastry makes *strudel* a not-so-smart alternative.

SCANDINAVIAN

SOME SMART CHOICES

With its very abbreviated growing seasons, Scandinavia—the countries of Norway, Sweden, Denmark, and Finland—doesn't feature a tremendous array of vegetables on its menus.

Salmon is rich in vitamin A and beneficial omega-3 fatty acids and is often found on Scandinavian menus.

TIP

Smorgasbord is a buffet groaning with an incredible array of meats and salads. These are fine if you go light on the sauced and creamed meats and heavy on the vegetables. Take a small plate to help control portions.

WHAT'S IN IT?

Proximity to the ocean in many places means that fish—and particularly salmon, herring, cod, and arctic char—are extremely common on Scandinavian tables.

Kottbular—fat- and calorie-laden Swedish meatballs.

WHAT'S THE BEST?

● *Vasterbotten.* A strong, aged cheese with the texture of Cheddar and a bite reminiscent of Parmesan; a little of this in a dish adds plenty of flavor.

● Norwegian salmon. If you think "smoked" when you hear Norwegian salmon, you're missing out. This deep red, finely textured fish is as flavorful as it is healthful.

WHAT'S NOT SO GOOD?

● *Gravlax.* In Swedish, the name means "buried salmon"—and it's covered in a mixture of sugar and salt (with a little dill). Most of the cure is rinsed off, but enough penetrates the flesh to cure it.

SMART CHOICES

▼▼▲ Root vegetables. Rutabagas are sometimes called swedes; this deep yellow vegetable is a good source of beta-carotene.

▼▼ Herring. As long as it isn't creamed, this fish is an excellent option. Herrings are quite high in fat—a 3-ounce serving supplies almost 10 grams—but about 15 percent of that is in the form of beneficial omega-3 fatty acids.

NOT-SO-SMART CHOICES

▲▲ Janson's Temptation. This is a mixture of potatoes and anchovies laced with cream.

▲ Toast skagen. Shrimp, onion, dill, and sometimes caviar are chopped finely and mixed with mayonnaise before mounding on toast.

▲▲▲ Kottbular. Swedish meatballs are most often a blend of beef, veal, and pork; they're combined with milk-soaked bread, onions, and egg, then sautéed and covered with gravy.

Rutabaga

RUSSIAN

● ●

SOME SMART CHOICES

*I*t's impossible to summarize *Russian cuisine in two pages, but restaurants that specialize in Russian food often include classic dishes on the menu.*

WHAT'S IN IT?

Vinegret isn't a vinegar-based salad dressing—it's a salad made of beets, potatoes, onions, and pickles, held together with mayonnaise.

Onion

Beets

Potato

WHAT'S THE BEST?

● Soups are a terrific choice. *Borscht*, made of fresh beets, may be served either hot or cold. It's garnished with a dollop of sour cream, but because it's made with broth, it makes a fairly low-fat and yet nutrient-rich start to a meal. Cucumber soup is another popular option.

Shashlik

WHAT'S NOT SO GOOD?

● *Coulibiac*, which is also known as *kulebiaka*, is a very rich dish that includes salmon, rice, hard-cooked eggs, mushrooms, and dill in a creamy sauce. It is cooked in either brioche dough or puff pastry.

NOT-SO-SMART CHOICES

▲▲ Chicken Kiev. Stuff a chicken breast with herb butter and seal it so that the butter can't escape, dip it in egg and bread crumbs, then sauté until crisp. Yes, it's as calorie-laden as it sounds. Cut into it carefully, as hot butter will spurt out.

▲▲ *Stroganoff*. Made by sautéing thin slices of beef tenderloin or top loin in butter with onion and mushroom, then combining with a sour-cream sauce, *stroganoff* is a rich, heavy dish.

▲ *Pelmeni*. If these dumplings (often stuffed with beef, veal, or chicken) are in a broth-based soup, they're acceptable; if they're an entrée served with sour cream and hot-sweet mustard, consider looking for a lower-fat dish.

▲▲ *Pirozhki*. These are akin to Poland's *pierogi*—rounds of dough stuffed most frequently with mashed potatoes; occasionally the potatoes are flavored with cheese or onions. *Pirozhki* are often served with butter, sour cream, or applesauce.

SMART CHOICES

▼ Shashlik. Skewered foods, most often meat but occasionally vegetables, can be either an appetizer or an entrée.

▼ *Basturma*. This air-dried beef has a texture not unlike a top-quality cured ham. Its flavor is slightly smoky, but it isn't as salty as hams generally are.

▼▼ Caviar. This comes in a dizzying array of prices from a variety of species of sturgeon. Caviar is high in fat and cholesterol, but it provides some vitamins A and D, and it supplies some carotenoid pigments, too.

MEZZE AND MIDDLE EASTERN

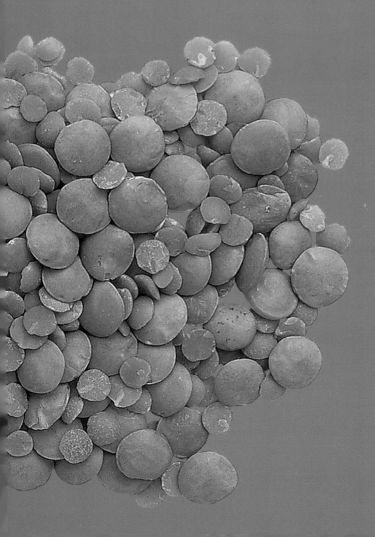

MEZZE AND MIDDLE EASTERN

With similarities to cuisines from Asia and Europe, culinary traditions from countries in the Middle East reflect these countries' historical importance as parts of traditional trade routes.

Several dishes are common to many countries, so there is considerable overlap among the cuisines on the following pages.

Mezze is a style of eating that is common throughout the Mediterranean. Not unlike tapas and antipasti, mezze involves many small dishes that can be served as hors d'oeuvres with cocktails or wine, as a first course, or as a delicious light meal. It's a marvelous introduction to an unfamiliar cuisine, or a good way to sample several favorites, if you are bewildered by the choice and aren't sure what to order.

135

TURKISH

● ● ●

SOME HEALTHFUL OPTIONS

Vegetables, some meat and dairy, and generous amounts of olive oil make Turkish cooking full of healthful choices.

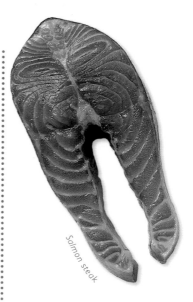

Salmon steak

TIP

● *Kofte* are small patties typically made of lamb. Sometimes they're fried; at other times they're grilled as kabobs. If the menu doesn't specify the cooking method, ask—fried *kofte* can be much higher in fat.

WHAT'S IN IT?

Turkey's long coastline means that seafood makes frequent appearances on menus. Shrimp, squid, sea bass, and salmon are baked, made into casseroles, or cubed and threaded onto skewers for kabobs.

WHAT'S THE BEST?

● Bulgur is a form of wheat; it contains both the germ and the bran. It's used in breads, but most often it's steamed and mixed with chopped tomatoes, mint, scallions, olive oil, and lemon and served as an appetizer or side dish called *bulgur pilaf.*

Bulgur wheat is full of fiber and makes a nutritious, nutty-flavored salad when combined with tomatoes, mint, scallions, and olive oil.

Fried eggplant served with chopped scallion and a dip often forms part of a Turkish mezze.

WHAT'S NOT SO GOOD?

● *Kalamar*, or squid, is frequently served deep-fried with a tartar sauce on the side.

● *Mucver* are zucchini pancakes often served as an appetizer. They're pan-fried in oil; zucchini doesn't absorb as much fat as eggplant does, but the fritters do absorb some.

SMART CHOICES

▼ Kabobs. Almost always meat (lamb, fish, and chicken are the most common; you might find beef, but never pork), but sometimes vegetables, the food is typically marinated in a mixture of lemon, olive oil, onion, and spices before grilling.

▼▲ *Mezair.* This condiment is not unlike salsa. It is made of tomatoes and garlic chopped with parsley and mint, spiked with lemon juice. It's a common accompaniment to bread and meat dishes.

▼ *Manti.* Beef-stuffed dumplings served with a garlicky yogurt sauce, *manti* can be steamed or poached.

▼▼ *Pathcan salatasi.* If you're an eggplant lover, look for this (usually under cold appetizers). It's most often made of broiled eggplant (not fried), puréed with red and green bell peppers, lemon juice, and spices.

NOT-SO-SMART CHOICES

▲▲▲ *Pideler.* Similar to pizza, *pideler* can be topped with chopped meat, pastrami, *kasar* (a Turkish cheese), vegetables, tomato sauce, or sausage. The crust is often thick, and it can be stuffed with feta cheese.

▲▲ *Tavuk sote.* This dish features chicken and vegetables that are cooked in butter, then topped with a butter sauce.

GREEK

● ● ● ●

MANY HEALTHFUL CHOICES

A warm, sunny climate, combined with an extensive coastline and little pastureland, mean that Greek cooking typically features plenty of nutritious vegetables, fish, and lamb.

WHAT'S IN IT?

Moussaka and *pastitsio* are both compared to lasagna. *Pastitsio* includes pasta and lamb; moussaka features layers of eggplant, potato, lamb, and tomatoes; both are sauced with a yogurt béchamel and baked.

WHAT'S THE BEST?

● Perhaps no other cuisine reveres the olive in quite the way that Greek cooking does. The fruit finds its way into many dishes, and olive oil is the primary cooking fat.

● Yogurt is used as a base for several condiments, most famously *tzatziki*, a blend of grated or finely minced cucumber, garlic, and rich, whole-milk yogurt that is served with many Greek dishes.

Tzatziki and cucumber salad

Moussaka is one Greek dish that is now known worldwide.

Dolmades *may be made with either grape or cabbage leaves, and filled with a range of ingredients.*

WHAT'S NOT SO GOOD?

● *Avegolemono* is both a soup and a sauce. They're both quite rich and include egg, chicken broth, and lemon, though the sauce is considerably thicker. The soup may include chicken meat, and often incorporates rice.

TIP

● Dips are often part of a mezze platter, but watch out for taramasalata if you're controlling your carb intake. Usually described as "caviar mousse," this is often made with bread crumbs that have been soaked in milk.

SMART CHOICES

▲▼ *Stifado.* This is a hearty baked stew made of meat—usually lamb, though beef and rabbit are not uncommon—tomatoes, onions, and wine, seasoned with garlic, cinnamon, and oregano.

▼▼ *Souvlaki.* Chunks of lamb are marinated in a zesty blend of olive oil, lemon, oregano, and spices, then skewered and grilled. *Souvlaki* may include bell peppers or other vegetables, too.

▼ *Dolmades.* As an appetizer, *dolmades* are grape leaves wrapped around seasoned rice mixed with tomatoes and herbs; as an entrée, it may be cabbage leaves stuffed with spicy ground lamb.

NOT-SO-SMART CHOICES

▲▲▲ Phyllo or fillo, is thin sheets of pastry rolled with butter. It's used in the dessert *baklava*, as well as in *spanikopita* (spinach pie) and *tiropita* (cheese pie)—two incredibly rich, incredibly high-fat, high-carb dishes.

▲▲ *Gyro.* This popular sandwich is made of ground lamb, molded around a spit before roasting. The meat is cut into thin slices, then stuffed into pitas, topped with vegetables, and drizzled with *tzatziki.* The lamb isn't often trimmed of fat before grinding.

EASTERN MEDITERRANEAN

● ● ● ●

MANY HEALTHFUL CHOICES

Many of the dishes that are found on Syrian, Lebanese, and Israeli menus are similar to each other—and to Greek, Turkish, and other Mediterranean cusines as well.

TIP

● If you're at all squeamish about raw meat, ask about *kibbeh* before ordering it. These patties can vary widely, but are often made with bulgur and lamb or other meat—and the meat may well be raw.

WHAT'S IN IT?

Baba ghanoush (sometimes spelled *gannouj* or *ghannouj*) is a dip that is classically made of roasted eggplant, as well as tahini (ground sesame seeds) and olive oil, among other ingredients. If the eggplant is cubed and tossed with olive oil before roasting, the dip can be surprisingly high in fat.

WHAT'S THE BEST?

● Legumes are common in Mediterranean dishes. Lentils, chickpeas, and white beans (among others) provide protein, complex carbohydrate, fiber, and a variety of vitamins and minerals.

WHAT'S NOT SO GOOD?

● Legumes are often cooked by high-fat methods, or are sometimes mixed with high-carbohydrate foods. Pay attention to cooking methods—or ask about them—as well as to ingredient descriptions on menus.

Chickpeas

Red and green lentils

Hummus

LEFT *Falafel are small, deep-fried patties made of highly spiced ground chickpeas.*

SMART CHOICES

▼▼ Tabbouleh. Sometimes spelled *tabouli*, this dish is made of bulgur, a type of cracked wheat, mixed with tomatoes, scallions or onions, mint, parsley, olive oil, and lemon juice. It's typically served cold as an appetizer.

▼▲ Hummus. High in fiber and complex carbohydrates, hummus is made of mashed or puréed cooked chickpeas mixed with tahini, olive oil, lemon juice, garlic, and spices such as cumin.

▼ Fattoush. A salad made of bread, cucumbers, scallions or onions, and tomato, tossed with a garlic-lemon dressing, *fattoush* is served as an accompaniment to grilled lamb or chicken, or is served with bread.

NOT-SO-SMART CHOICES

▲▲ *Shawarma.* This Middle Eastern version of Greece's *gyro* can be made with lamb, chicken, or veal. It may be spread with hummus or a spicy yogurt sauce, and is usually stuffed into a pita or may be wrapped in *lavash*, a type of flatbread.

▲ Falafel. Made by cooking and then mashing or grinding chickpeas, mixing them with seasonings, then forming them into balls or croquettes and frying, falafel can be served as an appetizer with a yogurt dipping sauce, or tucked into a pita bread.

MOROCCAN AND NORTH AFRICAN

● ● ● ●

MANY HEALTHFUL CHOICES

*A*s with other culinary traditions throughout the Middle East and Asia, the cuisine of Morocco and North Africa reflects the Islamic proscription on eating pork.

Raisins

TIP

● Although couscous looks like a grain, it's made from semolina, the same flour that pasta is made from. Couscous itself is high in refined carbohydrate; the term can also refer to dishes made with couscous. Berber couscous, for example, is made with no fewer than seven vegetables.

WHAT'S IN IT?

Lamb and chicken are the two most common meats; legumes, particularly lentils and chickpeas, are also popular. Moroccan cuisine is different from other cooking styles that border the Mediterranean, however; it combines savory ingredients with dried fruits, so many dishes have a hint of sweetness.

WHAT'S THE BEST?

● *Tagine* is the name of a stewlike dish, as well as the conical clay pot in which it's cooked. Made of vegetables, lamb, fish, or chicken combined with any number of ingredients—olives and preserved lemon; garlic, saffron, and onion; carrots, apple, okra, and dried currants—*tagines* are more savory than spicy.

WHAT'S NOT SO GOOD?

● Phyllo (or fillo) is used in many dishes—the "pot pie" *bastilla*, as well as *brek*, a deep-fried turnover filled with highly seasoned meat or fish. *Brek* (sometimes spelled *borek*) is often served with *harissa*, a very hot sauce made of fiery chiles.

Couscous

Lamb and apricot tagine is full of protein and iron.

SMART CHOICES

▼▼ *Mechoui.* Often available only as an advance order, *mechoui* is lamb that has been marinated in saffron-infused red wine, then slow-roasted, braised, or baked until succulent and tender—usually for six or so hours.

▼▲ Salads. Whether *chermoula* (spiced carrots), *immouzer* (lettuce, tomatoes, and cucumbers), or *bakoula* (spinach with cumin and paprika), vegetable dishes are high in flavor, yet low in calories and fat.

▼▲ *Harira.* A soup made of lentils, chickpeas, and beef flavored with tomatoes and onions, *harira* makes an excellent beginning to a meal.

NOT-SO-SMART CHOICES

▲ *Bastilla.* Made by stewing pheasant or chicken in a spicy saffron broth, then combining this with almonds and cinnamon and covering with phyllo, like a type of pot pie, *bastilla* can be high in refined carbohydrates. It's sometimes spelled *b'steeya* or even *pastilla.*

▲ *Arobi.* A Moroccan-style mixed grill, *arobi* features grilled chicken, lamb chops, seasoned ground beef patties, and sausage. Although it's fine if you're following a controlled-carb eating plan, it may also be high in fat.

COOKING OF
THE AMERICAS

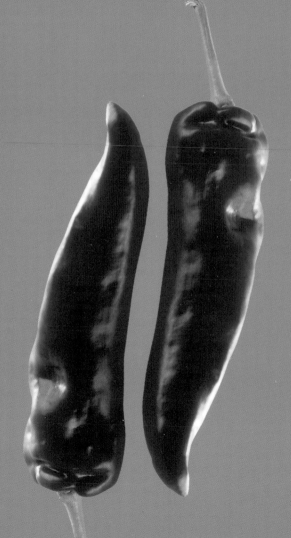

COOKING OF
THE AMERICAS

*American cooking is a melting pot. From
the pampas of Argentina to the plains of the
United States, native ingredients and dishes have
been adapted by immigrants.*

Whether you're making a meal of feijoada
*or of Dungeness crab, there are words to
look for—and look out for—on menus.
They vary by type of cuisine (sometimes the
same term means different things in different
places) and are outlined in the following pages.*

*Many of the not-so-smart choices are
favorites and classics. Should you never order
them because they're high in saturated fat or
refined carbohydrates? In a word, no. But if
you decide to indulge, make sure that the
rest of your meals and snacks that day
(or surrounding days) are smart choices.*

BRAZILIAN
● ● ●
SOME HEALTHFUL OPTIONS

B *razilian cooking is a delicious blend of Portuguese, African, and Native American ingredients and techniques.*

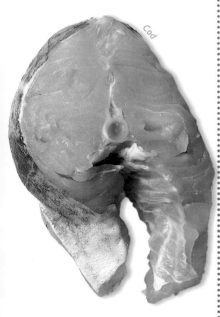

Cod

WHAT'S THE BEST?

● Brazilian food is a protein lover's paradise. Meats and seafood are often of excellent quality and are expertly prepared. *Churrasco* is a type of Brazilian barbecue prepared on skewers. Often, waiters roam the restaurant and offer cuts to diners.

WHAT'S NOT SO GOOD?

● *Farinha* is cassava meal. This incredibly starchy tuber is ground and then toasted; it is then sprinkled over most dishes. *Farofa* is made by toasting the *farinha* in butter or by mixing it with boiling water until it is a paste.

WHAT'S IN IT?

Cream isn't used often, but watch out for dende oil, or palm oil. Dende oil is easily identifiable by its orange color; it is very high in saturated fat. Coconut milk is also used in many dishes; it's preferable to coconut cream.

Dende oil

Coconut

Coconut milk

Coconut milk is refreshing and adds flavor to many dishes, and is less fatty than coconut cream.

SMART CHOICES

▼ Look for *grelhado* or *grelhada*. Foods prepared in this manner are broiled or grilled.

▼ *Feijoada*. Often called the Brazilian national dish, this stew features black beans and smoked meats like pork, beef, and sausage—it can be high in fat, so moderate the amount of meat you eat. Black beans are high in folate, fiber, and protein.

▼▲ *Caldo verde*. A Portuguese soup made with potatoes, sausage, and plenty of collard greens, this filling dish is a meal-in-a-bowl.

▼▲ Salads. Although some Brazilian restaurants feature mixed greens, you may find salads of vegetables or seafood sprinkled with vinegar. They aren't salads in the traditional sense, but they are refreshing between courses.

NOT-SO-SMART CHOICES

▲▲ Beware the phrase "Bahian sauce"—dende oil (see opposite) is often an ingredient.

▲▲ *Vatapa*. A stew made of fish or chicken, this also includes dried shrimp, peanuts, palm oil, and coconut milk.

▲ *Linguiça frita. Linguiça* is a deliciously spicy Portuguese sausage, but it's very high in fat. Ask exactly what "*frita*" means—if it's fried in additional oil, then pass on it.

Shrimp

PERUVIAN

● ● ●

SOME HEALTHFUL OPTIONS

High elevations, little pastureland, and a long coastline mean that Peru's indigenous cuisine is light in beef and high in nutritious fish.

TIP

● Seafood, including scallops (*conchitas*), shrimp, crayfish, sea bass (*corvina*), and abalone are common in Peruvian kitchens.

WHAT'S IN IT?

Although you'll find some Spanish influence on Peruvian recipes, you'll also find similarities to Mexican cooking. *Tamal*, *rellenos*, and *empanadas* are common appetizers.

WHAT'S THE BEST?

● *Ceviche*—or, as it's often spelled on Peruvian menus, *cebiche*—is made by marinating different types of fish and seafood in lime juice. The acid from the citrus "cooks" the fish, while seasonings in the marinade infuse it with flavor.

WHAT'S NOT SO GOOD?

● *Ceviche* isn't cooked in the traditional sense. Because there's no heat to kill any bacteria that may be present in the fish, order it at a restaurant that you trust to have impeccably fresh fish and impeccably high standards of cleanliness.

Shrimp

Scallops

Scallops and shrimp feature prominently on Peruvian menus and, like all shellfish, are rich in protein.

Like all white fish, sea bass is an excellent source of lean protein.

SMART CHOICES

▼ *Anticucho.* These grilled skewers are traditionally made with beef heart, but chicken and fish (particularly swordfish and bonito) are also common.

▼ *Aji* and *rocoto*. *Aji* means "hot pepper"; *rocoto* is a type of chile that is somewhat hotter than a jalapeño. They add plenty of flavor and contain no fat, but if you're not a fan of spicy foods you may want to avoid dishes with these terms.

▼▲ *Tacu-tacu.* This is rice and beans; they're typically cooked separately, and then combined. Often they're then cooked again, being mashed into a patty.

NOT-SO-SMART CHOICES

▲ *Lomo saltado.* Thinly sliced steak, sautéed with potatoes, onions, and tomatoes, this is often served with rice as well, making it extra-high in carbohydrates.

▲▲ *Chaufa.* Reflecting the Chinese influence in Peru, *chaufa* is a version of fried rice. It includes chunks of ham, seafood, peas, and eggs; the rice is often clumpier than it is in Chinese fried rice.

▲ *Jalea.* If the menu doesn't specify how this is prepared, ask. *Jalea* is a seafood combination platter; it's usually deep-fried.

▲▲ *Chupe.* This hearty stew is a meal-in-a-bowl—it often includes crayfish, potatoes, and rice, as well as plenty of cream or cheese (usually *queso blanco*).

ARGENTINIAN

● ● ●

SOME HEALTHFUL OPTIONS

*A*rgentina has a large Italian population, so don't be surprised if you see pasta, polenta, antipasti, and similar dishes on Argentinian menus.

Sweet potato

TIP

● If you're splurging on a steak, don't forget to watch portion sizes. Many steaks weigh a pound or more. If the cut you want comes only in a 16- or 18-ounce size, plan on taking half home.

Spaghetti

WHAT'S IN IT?

Argentina is justifiably proud of its beef, and most Argentinian restaurants are steakhouses. Beef, fried potatoes, and a variety of salads are menu mainstays.

Argentina is renowned for its beef, and steak comes in all forms and sizes.

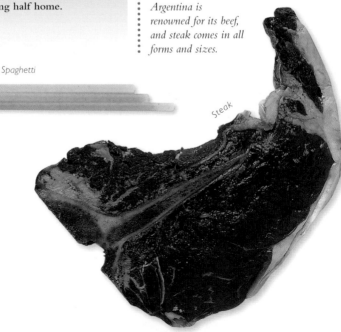

Steak

Chorizo

Salmon

WHAT'S THE BEST?

● Can't make up your mind? *Churrasco* is a mixed grill—a variety of cuts, including beef, pork, and sausages— served with *chimichurri* sauce. This green sauce gets its coloring from parsley and its addictive flavor from plenty of garlic, vinegar, and spices.

WHAT'S NOT SO GOOD?

● Sausages. If you know you're getting a *churrasco*, skip the sausage appetizers. *Chorizo* (a spicy pork sausage), *morcilla* (blood sausage), and *salchicha* (a smoked and dried pork sausage) are all quite high in fat.

CUBAN

● ● ●

SOME HEALTHFUL OPTIONS

Cumin

Lime

Garlic

Rich in flavors, Cuban cooking blends elements of Spanish and Caribbean cuisines, and then adds elements all its own.

WHAT'S IN IT?

Garlic, cumin, and lime or sour orange juice are the defining flavors of Cuban food. They're the primary ingredients in *adobo*, the Cuban marinade for steaks, seafood, and poultry. When combined in slightly different proportions and cooked, they become *mojo*, a sauce that adorns vegetables, steaks and seafoods, and sandwiches.

WHAT'S THE BEST?

● Black beans. More common in Cuba than beans of other colors, *frijoles negros* supply fiber, folate, and flavor, with very little fat. They're an excellent source of protein and complex carbohydrate. Frequently served as a side dish, black beans are also an ingredient in many different Cuban recipes.

Cumin, a pungent spice, lime, and garlic are common ingredients of Cuban sauces and marinades.

TIP

● Watch out for *mofongo*. This side dish is usually described as mashed plantains—sounds benign enough, right? In fact, the plantains are typically fried before being mashed, and the dish often includes salt pork as a flavoring.

SMART CHOICES

▼ *Ropa vieja.* Once you get past the unappetizing name (it means "old clothes"), *ropa vieja* is delicious. It's shredded beef (often flank steak) that's cooked with onions and peppers in a tomato sauce.

▼ *Picadillo.* Popular throughout Latin America and the Caribbean, *picadillo* is ground beef or pork, seasoned with tomatoes, garlic, onions, and raisins. In Cuba, it's usually spooned around a mound of rice, with black beans on the side. (It can also be used as a stuffing.)

NOT-SO-SMART CHOICES

▲▲ *Arroz con pollo.* This chicken-and-rice dish is a stripped-down version of paella that is often made with skin-on chicken parts rather than diced, skinless chicken. In skin-on form, it is much higher in fat.

▲ *Salpicon.* This salad of diced meat and cooked vegetables is tossed with mayonnaise.

▲▲ Cuban sandwiches. Roast pork, ham, Swiss cheese, and pickles—sometimes buttered and grilled, but always pressed—make for a sandwich that is high in fat and sodium.

WHAT'S NOT SO GOOD?

● Yellow rice. If this gets its color only from *annatto* (a natural food coloring, sometimes called *achiote*), it's a fine addition to your menu. However, yellow rice often contains a seasoning blend that is very high in sodium.

When ground beef or pork is combined with onions, raisins, and tomatoes, plus garlic, it makes the Cuban dish known as picadillo.

Onion

Raisins

Tomato

153

JAMAICAN
● ● ●
SOME HEALTHFUL OPTIONS

Jamaican food gets its fire from country peppers—they're as hot as habaneros and Scotch bonnets— and its sweet counterpoint from coconut and fruits.

TIP

● Rice and peas is a common dish, but isn't always made with peas. Although gungo peas are used in the Caribbean, kidney beans are often used instead.

Kidney beans

Plantain

WHAT'S IN IT?

Jerk is probably Jamaica's best-known culinary contribution, but if you're confused about what it is, that's not surprising. Jerk can be a dry rub, a wet marinade, a method of cooking, or the finished dish. Jerk seasoning is as individual as the cook who makes it, but includes chiles, spices, and herbs, and is always very spicy.

WHAT'S THE BEST?

● Sweet potatoes. These deep-orange vegetables are lower in carbs and higher in nutrients—particularly beta-carotene—than most other starchy vegetables. Sweet potato is a much more nutritious option than plantain, yuca, or boniato.

WHAT'S NOT SO GOOD?

● *Yuca frituras.* Yuca would never be mistaken for a nutrient-rich vegetable, but deep-fry it to make fritters and you've really done a number on it.

Tostones are fried chips made of green plantains; like potato chips, they're usually served with a dip or a sauce. They're utterly addictive, so best to order them with a group.

Cayenne

SMART CHOICES

▼▼ Curry and coconut. These are two common seasonings in Jamaican cooking. Coconut milk, the liquid extracted from coconut meat, is fairly low in fat and carbohydrate. However, coconut cream is high in fat, and cream of coconut (which is used in tropical cocktails) is high in both fat and sugar.

▼▼▼ *Calaloo*. Although spellings vary, this green, spinach-like vegetable is a popular side dish and an ingredient in many stuffings.

▼ Fish. *Escovitch* is the Jamaican version of *escabeche*, a dish similar to *ceviche*, in which chunks of shellfish and fish are marinated and chilled for hours.

Sweet potatoes blend well with herbs and spices, and are packed full of beta-carotene.

NOT-SO-SMART CHOICES

▲▲ Oxtail. You'll find oxtail soup and stews on plenty of Jamaican menus, but be cautious—this cut of meat can be very fatty.

▲ Pineapple. This adds flavor and sweetness to many dishes—and its acidic juice is used in many marinades—but it and many other tropical fruits are high in sugars.

▲▲ *Roti*. Similar to a burrito, this flat Indian bread can be filled with a number of foods. Choose wisely, so it doesn't become a dietary disaster.

CARIBBEAN

● ● ●

SOME HEALTHFUL OPTIONS

*A*lthough each island has a unique style, there are many overlapping elements in Caribbean cooking. European influences abound, as do the tastes of Africa and Asia.

Avocado

WHAT'S IN IT?

Be warned: sometimes the same word means different things. In Cuban cooking, *adobo* is a marinade made of garlic, cumin, and lime. Puerto Rican menus use the term to describe a seasoning blend of salt with pepper, cumin, and garlic.

WHAT'S THE BEST?

● Goat meat can be gamy, but most of the meat served in restaurants is from kid. Its flavor is similar to lamb's, and it is significantly lower in calories and fat than lamb, beef, or chicken.

Chiles

Crab

WHAT'S NOT SO GOOD?

● Meat patties and fishcakes are especially common on menus in casual restaurants. Depending on the meat used, whether any fillers (such as bread crumbs) are included, what binders (such as eggs or mayonnaise) are used in the fishcakes, and what seasonings are added, these can be high in fat, carbohydrate, and sodium.

SMART CHOICES

▼ *Asopao.* This Puerto Rican dish is a soupy stew made of chicken, shrimp or lobster, and rice.

▼ *La parilla* and *la brasa.* Meaning "grilled" and "charbroiled," these are words to look for if the menu isn't written in a language with which you're entirely conversant.

▼▲ Avocados. Do you think of these as fattening fruits to avoid while dieting? Think again. Avocados are certainly high in fat, but it's mostly monounsaturated, which has been shown to lower cholesterol. They're also high in fiber, folate, vitamin B6, and iron.

▼▼▲ Seafood. Whether you opt for king fish, scallops, red snapper, crabs, or conch, seafood abounds. Just choose grilled, broiled, or baked to ensure that you make the most of its low-fat makeup.

NOT-SO-SMART CHOICES

▲▲ Seafood. If you're hungry for fish, skip the fried fritters, the crispy cakes, and the creamy chowders.

▲ Curried crab and dumplings. Curries are popular on former British colonies like Jamaica and Trinidad and Tobago. In the Caribbean, they're likely to include coconut milk rather than yogurt, though, and can be high in fat.

▲ Drunken chicken. Made of cubed chicken, vegetables, lime, rum, and sugar, this dish can be quite high in carbohydrate.

MEXICAN

● ● ●

SOME HEALTHFUL OPTIONS

You're more likely to get an authentic—and more healthful—meal at a small or independent Mexican restaurant than you are at a large chain.

TIP

● The salsa that many restaurants bring while you're waiting for your food is full of vitamins and low in calories, fat, and carbohydrates, but pass on the fried tortilla chips that accompany it. Ask for baked chips or tortillas—or for fresh vegetables like bell peppers and jicama—instead.

WHAT'S IN IT?

The building blocks of Mexican food are corn, rice and beans, vegetables (especially tomatoes), tortillas, and a fresh cheese called *queso blanco*; seasonings include cumin, fresh and dried chiles, and cilantro. When you add lots of Cheddar or Monterey Jack, meat, and sour cream, that's when you add the fat and calories.

WHAT'S THE BEST?

● Condiments. *Pico de gallo*, guacamole, ranchero sauce, chile sauce, *salsa verde*, and salsas made with a variety of fresh vegetables and fruits add flavor without adding much fat or carbohydrate.

WHAT'S NOT SO GOOD?

● Condiments. Sour cream, *chile con queso*, and cheesy dips and sauces are high in calories and fat. A small spoonful of sour cream can help tame the heat of some dishes, but steer clear of big dollops.

Mexican green, avocado, and herb salsas.

Guacamole is a nutritious mix of avocados, garlic, and tomatoes.

SMART CHOICES

▼▼ Fajitas. Build your own entrée, loading up the vegetables. Because fajitas may be sautéed, use your fork to lift them out of the oil, giving them a gentle shake to rid them of any excess.

▼▼ Soft tacos. Because tacos are often made with small tortillas, they're lower in fat, calories, and carbs than other Mexican entrées. Soft tacos are made with flour tortillas; because these aren't fried, they are lower in fat.

▼▼ Fish tacos. If the fish is grilled rather than fried, these are an excellent choice, even in a fried corn tortilla (corn tortillas are lower in carbohydrate than flour tortillas are).

NOT-SO-SMART CHOICES

▲▲ *Chimichangas.* Take a burrito - size tortilla or two, stuff with a few servings worth of cheese, meat or poultry, rice, beans, and vegetables, and then deep-fry. Serve with sour cream and refried beans—and watch the calories soar.

▲▲ Taco salad. Calling this a salad is stretching it—it might contain a bit more lettuce than the tacos do, but not much. If it's served in a deep-fried tortilla "bowl," resist the temptation to eat it. It's astonishingly high in fat and calories.

▲▲ *Chiles rellenos.* Cheese-stuffed, batter-dipped, deep-fried chiles, and their smaller cousin the jalapeño pepper, are a nutritional nightmare.

MEXICAN

SOME HEALTHFUL OPTIONS

*A*uthentic Mexican food isn't always spicy-hot—a more accurate term might be complex. A variety of spices, ranging from cumin to cinnamon and even unsweetened cocoa, provide a depth of flavor.

Rice and beans, flavored with a variety of herbs and spices, make a delicious dish for vegetarians and nonvegetarians alike.

Cinnamon

WHAT'S IN IT?

Mole is a richly flavored sauce that is typically served with poultry. It includes garlic, chocolate, cinnamon, cloves, and sometimes raisins.

WHAT'S THE BEST?

● Splitting entrées is a wise idea, particularly when portions are enormous. If your dining companions aren't interested in sharing, cut your serving in half when it's placed in front of you, and plan to take one half home for another meal.

WHAT'S NOT SO GOOD?

● *Quesadillas* are a sort of grilled cheese sandwich made with tortillas instead of bread. Most restaurants make them by frying the flour tortillas in oil, then piling on the cheese. When topped with a huge scoop of sour cream, these are very high in fat.

SMART CHOICES

▼▼ *Posole* is a hearty stew made of pork, hominy, onions, garlic, and chiles. It can be served with chopped tomatoes, onion, cilantro, and onions on the side, which you can add to suit your taste.

▼▲ Rice and beans. Looking for a simple, nutritious light meal or side dish? Spring for rice and beans— white rice is lower in sodium than yellow rice, and black beans are higher in nutrients than red beans or refried beans.

▲ Guacamole. If you shun this because it's high in fat, you're not doing yourself any favors. It is high in monounsaturated fat, which can help to lower cholesterol levels, and also high in fiber, iron, and folate.

NOT-SO-SMART CHOICES

▲▲▲ *Tamales*. A dough made of *masa* (a type of corn) is wrapped around chopped meat and vegetables, then the dough is wrapped in a corn husk and steamed. *Tamales* are usually savory, but some are sweet; they are quite high in carbohydrate, but their fat and calorie content depends on the filling.

▲▲ Enchiladas. Although flour tortillas are fairly low in fat, they are often dipped in oil to soften them. Although the fillings aren't usually bad, there's often an unconscionable amount of cheese coating them.

▲ *Refritos*. Most often made with red beans or pinto beans, *refritos* are cooked, then mashed and fried, traditionally in lard.

CALIFORNIA AND THE PACIFIC COAST

● ● ● ●

MANY HEALTHFUL OPTIONS

When France's nouvelle cuisine met California's pristine ingredients in the 1970s, "California cooking" was born and began to spread up the coast and across the country.

TIP

● In addition to French influences, you'll find that Italian ingredients and techniques are used (especially in San Francisco), as well as Spanish, Mexican, Japanese, Chinese, and Vietnamese.

WHAT'S IN IT?

With several thousand miles of coastline, fish and shellfish are hugely popular appetizers and entrées. Often grilled over wood-burning fires, they are prepared simply to make the most of the foods' natural flavors.

WHAT'S THE BEST?

● Mild climates mean that fruits and vegetables can be used all year round, virtually fresh from the earth. When foods don't have to be shipped cross-country—or imported—they are higher in vitamins and in flavor.

WHAT'S NOT SO GOOD?

● Caesar salad was invented by Caesar Cardini in Tijuana back in the 1920s, but it was popularized in Hollywood. Sometimes the dressing contains raw or barely cooked eggs, which can harbor bacteria.

A seafood salad makes the most of the Pacific coast's rich sea life and makes a delicious summer dish.

Grilled vegetables sound appetizing and nutritious, but watch that they aren't dripping in fat.

SMART CHOICES

▼▲ Salmon. The northern waters of the Pacific are home to Chinook and Alaskan king salmon, large fish with vermillion flesh and an incomparable flavor. They're in season only briefly, so make sure you take advantage of them when they are.

▼▼ Crab. From the Dungeness crab so beloved in San Francisco to Alaskan king crab with its foot-long legs, crab is exceptionally low in fat, particularly saturated fat. It's often served with drawn butter, but skip this and let the flavor of the seafood stand on its own.

NOT-SO-SMART CHOICES

▲ Grilled vegetables. This healthy-sounding dish can be a fat-trap. The vegetables all too often aren't the most nutrient-rich ones and are often swimming in oil. Eggplant (which soaks up oil like a sponge), mushrooms, yellow squash, and zucchini are the most common and, with the exception of zucchini, aren't known for their vitamin content.

▲▲ Dinner salads. A small green salad to begin or end a meal is one thing, but a massive salad loaded with meat, cheese, croutons, crumbled bacon, and often tossed with a ½ cup—or more—of dressing is something else entirely. It isn't unusual for salads to be significantly higher in fat and calories than a cheeseburger.

SOUTH-WESTERN/ TEX-MEX

● ● ●

SOME HEALTHFUL OPTIONS

*S*trong similarities to Mexican cooking, combined with plenty of Texas beef, make Tex-Mex food a perennial favorite.

TIP

● Sour cream has a place on Tex-Mex tables, but it's a small one. Dairy products contain a protein that can neutralize the mouth-on-fire feeling from eating super-spicy foods.

Tomatillos may look like green tomatoes, but they're actually a relative of the Cape gooseberry.

WHAT'S IN IT?

A tremendous variety of chiles are used in Tex-Mex cooking, from the mild poblanos and anchos to jalapeños and chipotles and the incendiary habaneros.

WHAT'S THE BEST?

● Have you tried *jicama*? This looks like a raw potato, but its flavor is quite sweet and its flesh crunchy, yet juicy. *Jicama* is very low in carbohydrates.

● *Tomatillos* look like small green tomatoes in a papery husk. They're integral in *salsa verde*, a mild sauce used for dipping or to top enchiladas.

WHAT'S NOT SO GOOD?

● The name means "little donkey" in Spanish, but most burritos are anything but small. Most are as long as a forearm and at least as big round, and are overstuffed with too much meat, cheese, rice, and beans.

Chiles abound in Tex-Mex and south-western cooking.

SMART CHOICES

▼ Chili. If you're watching your carbs, authentic Texas-style chili is perfect. Made of chopped sirloin, spices, and broth, a "bowl of red" contains neither beans nor tomatoes.

▼▲ *Los Dos*. Keeping tabs on your fat grams? Rice and beans—*los dos* ("the two")—are often very low-fat and they combine to provide all the amino acids necessary for complete protein. Be sure to order an unseasoned rice, and beans that aren't refried.

▼▼▼ Lime. Sweet yet acidic, limes provide a delectable counterpoint to plenty of dishes. Chile-lime and tequila-lime chicken are high-flavor entrées.

NOT-SO-SMART CHOICES

▲▲▲ Nachos. Fried tortilla chips, mounded on a platter, then covered with chili, cheese, meat, and any other number of high-fat, high-carb toppings. If you must get these, split them among a large group.

▲▲▲ *Flautas*. A cross between a taco and a *chimichanga*, *flautas* are made by stuffing a corn tortilla with meat, cheese, and other fillings, then deep-frying it.

▲ Dips. Unless you opt for guacamole and salsa, or for *pico de gallo*, skip the dip. Bean dips and cheese dips are both high in harmful fats and calories.

CREOLE AND CAJUN

● ● ●

SOME HEALTHFUL OPTIONS

F rench influence is strong in Creole and Cajun cooking; you'll also find elements of Spanish and African cooking, as well as some Italian-inspired dishes.

TIP

● Creole cooking is the more refined of the two cuisines—it's the city cousin, if you will, to Cajun's no less flavorful but somewhat more rustic cooking. Creole restaurants often have classic French dishes such as *Filet Bearnaise*, Chicken *Bonne Femme*, and *Poisson Meunière* on the menu.

WHAT'S IN IT?

The two cornerstones that flavor virtually every dish are roux, a blend of flour and butter that is cooked to varying degrees of brownness, and the "holy trinity" of sautéed celery, onions, and green bell peppers.

A Cajun-spiced seafood stir-fry with noodles.

WHAT'S THE BEST?

● Crawfish look like tiny lobsters and have a sweet, succulent flesh. They're prepared in a variety of ways, but the two most *common—étouffée* and as Cajun popcorn—are neither low-fat nor low-carb.

WHAT'S NOT SO GOOD?

● Blackened foods were so popular in the 1980s that they became a cliché. When they're prepared authentically, though, they're low in fat, calories, and carbs. The food is rubbed with a blend of seasonings, then seared in a very, very hot cast-iron skillet. The spices and heat combine to form the characteristic crust, instead of flour and fat.

SMART CHOICES

▲ Shrimp Creole. The spicy tomato sauce in which the shrimp is simmered is high in lycopene, a potent antioxidant carotenoid.

▲ Red beans and rice. This dish isn't completely low-fat—it often includes spicy andouille sausage, bacon, or pork hocks—but it's one of the more nutritious options on most menus.

▼ Jambalaya. Although the jury's out on where the name of this dish came from, most agree that it always contains rice—but after that anything goes. Depending on what else goes into the pot, this dish can be a lean option.

Some jambalaya dishes are more nutritious, and less fatty, than others—one made with sausage will be on the high-fat side.

NOT-SO-SMART CHOICES

▲▲▲ Sandwiches. From the massive *muffaletta* (8–9 inches in diameter, filled with cold cuts and mozzarella) to the po' boy (fried oysters or other seafood, slathered with *remoulade* and tucked into a baguette), sandwiches are almost always high in calories, fat, and carbs.

▲▲ *Etouffée*. French for "smothered," Cajun *étouffée* is a thick, spicy stew that gets its deep color from a dark brown roux, or butter-and-flour mixture. It's typically made with crawfish and served over rice.

▲▲ Sausages. Andouille and boudin are two of the sausages that define Creole and Cajun cooking. They're acceptable in small amounts, but can be quite high in fat. Boudin is often made with rice.

SOUTHERN

● ● ●

SOME HEALTHFUL OPTIONS

*W*ith a geography that spans both coastal lowlands and high mountain ranges, the South has a diverse and delicious culinary tradition.

TIP

● Soft-shell crabs are delicious, highly perishable, and in season only briefly in the spring. They're most often dusted with flour and then pan-fried, so they aren't the most nutritious dish you'll find. If you're a fan, plan to eat moderately the day before or after you indulge.

WHAT'S IN IT?

Corn bread is a common accompaniment in the South, and it differs from Yankee corn bread in two distinct ways. Southern corn bread is often made with white cornmeal, not yellow, and it is rarely sweetened.

WHAT'S THE BEST?

● Believe it or not, fried chicken is okay—as long as you don't eat the skin. If it's fried properly, the meat itself absorbs very little of the fat in which it is fried.

● Spoonbread, grits, and corn bread are all made with cornmeal. Recipes vary, but they are all fairly low in fat; cornmeal is lower in carbohydrate than other grains are.

In the South, corn bread is usually a savory bread, often made with cheese as a component.

Surprisingly, fried chicken is not as bad for you as it may sound: it's high in protein and, as long as you remove the skin, not too high in fat.

WHAT'S NOT SO GOOD?

● Sweet potato casseroles—even if they aren't topped with tiny marshmallows—are often extremely high in sugar. Ask for a baked sweet potato instead.

● Hushpuppies. Because they are deep-fried, these cornmeal dumplings can be high in trans fats.

SMART CHOICES

▼ Country ham. Drier in texture and saltier in flavor than most commercial hams, authentic Southern country hams are comparable to Italy's *prosciutto* and Spain's *jamon serrano*.

▼▲ Greens. Turnip greens, collards, and dandelion greens are but three of the more common greens used in Southern cuisine. Typically cooked for a long time, often with bacon or ham hocks, these still retain considerable nutritional value.

▼▲ Hoppin' John. Made of cowpeas or pigeon peas and rice, and often seasoned with bacon, this dish is yet another nutrient-rich version of beans and rice.

NOT-SO-SMART CHOICES

▲▲▲ Hot Brown. This open-face sandwich, often called a Kentucky Hot Brown, consists of roasted turkey topped with cheese sauce and bacon.

▲ She-crab soup. An incredibly rich, creamy soup, this gets its name because roe is an ingredient.

▲▲ Biscuits. These contain considerably more fat than bread or rolls do. If you decide to indulge, resist the urge to split them open and slather them with butter.

BBQ

●

FEW HEALTHFUL OPTIONS

No one would ever argue that barbecue is health food, but there are some ways in which you can lessen the damage.

Barbecued chicken is delicious, but make sure it's properly cooked through and doesn't become too blackened.

TIP

● For tenderness and leanness, opt for baby back ribs. These pork ribs are from the loin. Their only drawback is that there often isn't much meat to them. Spareribs are from the belly, and country-style ribs are from the blade end of the loin. These are meatier, but they're also much fattier.

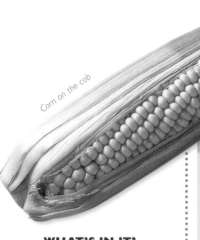

Corn on the cob

WHAT'S IN IT?

Barbecue means different things in different parts of the country, but one thing it shouldn't be confused with is grilling. Barbecue often involves large cuts of food cooked over low heat for a long time; grilling involves smaller pieces of food cooked briefly over a fairly high flame.

WHAT'S THE BEST?

● Dry barbecue is often lower in carbohydrate than wet barbecue. With dry barbecue, seasoning blends are rubbed onto the meat before they are cooked; the flavor permeates the meat.

WHAT'S NOT SO GOOD?

● Wet barbecue involves basting meats with sauce throughout the cooking. Sauce ingredients can vary considerably, but tomatoes, vinegar, and brown sugar or molasses are common ingredients. The meat is often served with sauce on the side, increasing the potential carb count.

SMART CHOICES

▼▼ Other foods. Barbecue joints often offer alternatives to barbecue. You might find chicken breast or even fish prepared in a variety of ways.

▼▼▲ Vegetables. Corn on the cob is high in two antioxidants that have been shown to prevent eye diseases. Collards are high in calcium. Coleslaw—if it's in a vinegar-based dressing rather than mayonnaise—can be high in nutrients, too.

▼▼ Barbecued chicken. If you're watching your fat grams, simply remove the skin. If you aren't concerned about sugars, ask for sauce on the side.

NOT-SO-SMART CHOICES

▲▲ Most sides. White bread, biscuits, or hushpuppies; French fries, onion rings, potato salad, pork and beans, and macaroni and cheese are commonly served to accompany barbecues. Few offer many nutritional benefits.

▲▲ Spareribs. You don't expect ribs to be low-fat—but spareribs and country-style ribs get about 70 percent of their calories from fat!

MIDWESTERN

SOME HEALTHFUL OPTIONS

*U*npretentious, hearty fare
*is the hallmark of the
Midwest—but that doesn't mean
unsophisticated. You'll find marvelous
flavors and ingredients.*

WHAT'S IN IT?

Although meat and potatoes are the
foundation of Midwestern food, fish
from lakes and rivers, world-class
cheeses, fruits, vegetables, and a
variety of grains are also common
ingredients of many dishes.

WHAT'S THE BEST?

● Cheese. Although it can be high in
fat, cheese is an excellent source of
calcium, and pungent varieties (such
as Maytag blue and extra-sharp
Cheddar) add considerable flavor,
even when used in small amounts.

WHAT'S NOT SO GOOD?

● *Wursts* and sausages are popular,
particularly in German and Polish
communities. Although most are of
excellent quality and don't contain
starchy fillers, they are often
extremely high in fat.

*Trout has a delicate flavor that is
perfectly complemented by a citrus
juice and fresh herbs.*

German sausage

Polish sausage

Wild rice

TIPS

● Just about every coffee shop, luncheonette, diner, and bakery sells cinnamon rolls the size of hubcaps, and not just for breakfast. Leave them in the display case.

● Although you'll find influences from recent immigrants from Mexico and Asia, Midwestern food is heavily influenced by German, Scandinavian, Polish, and Russian immigrants.

German and Polish sausage reflect the influx of immigrants to the Midwest; wild rice is another common ingredient.

SMART CHOICES

▼▼ Wild rice. Not always wild (it's often cultivated) and not a rice (it's an aquatic grass), wild rice is high in fiber and B vitamins and comparatively low in carbohydrates. It's often used in stuffings or is mixed with other grains to make a side dish.

▼▼▲ Think the best fish is available on the coasts? Think again. Perch, trout, walleyed pike, and whitefish are all delicious. Skip the all-you-can-eat fish fries and get yours baked or broiled instead.

NOT-SO-SMART CHOICES

▲▲ Meatloaf. A blend of high-fat ground beef, pork, and veal, meatloaf is often topped with gravy and is usually served with mashed potatoes, too.

▲▲▲ Most side dishes. From mashed potatoes and *pierogi* to the dumplings served with chicken and gelatin salads, side dishes are often a hit-or-miss proposition. (Sweet corn, salads made with whole grains, and garden-fresh vegetables are much better bets.)

NEW ENGLAND AND THE MID-ATLANTIC

● ● ● ●

MANY HEALTHFUL OPTIONS

From Maine lobster to Chesapeake Bay crab, there are both good and bad choices to be had among the states that border the Atlantic Ocean.

WHAT'S IN IT?

New England clam chowder and Manhattan clam chowder both contain clams, of course, as well as potatoes and aromatics like onions and celery. New England clam chowder is cream-based, though, whereas Manhattan clam chowder contains tomatoes.

TIP

● Seafood preparation is often extremely simple—it doesn't get more basic than boiling lobster—but watch out for the sauces and condiments. Drawn butter is a common accompaniment and it's all too easy to get more of it on a morsel of food than you mean to.

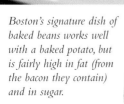

Boston's signature dish of baked beans works well with a baked potato, but is fairly high in fat (from the bacon they contain) and in sugar.

Lobster

Crab cakes contain copper and vitamin B3.

WHAT'S THE BEST?

● Properly prepared, crab cakes are very low in carbohydrate. The best ones have a bit of egg to hold them together, and perhaps some finely chopped vegetables or herbs to add flavor, but they don't include bread crumbs or other fillers.

WHAT'S NOT SO GOOD?

● Yankee pot roast with gravy can be extremely high in fat. The meats that work best for pot-roasting and braising are often fatty ones; if a restaurant isn't careful to skim the grease from the cooking liquid, the broth will be fatty, too. Be sure to trim any fat from the meat before eating.

SMART CHOICES

▼▼ Steamed seafood. Whether your choice is mussels, littlenecks, cherrystones, or another mollusk, most are steamed over a white-wine and herb-infused broth. Butter is occasionally added, so it's wise to ask.

▼▼ Portuguese influence. All along the New England coast, Portuguese immigrants settled. You'll find their influence in a variety of hearty fish-and-vegetable stews and other dishes.

NOT-SO-SMART CHOICES

▲▲▲ Chicken pot pie. Between the cream sauce and the pie crust or biscuit topping, pot pies are extremely high in fat. Depending on what vegetables are included, they can contain considerable carbs, too.

▲ Baked beans. Boston's quintessential dish is not a wise choice if you're watching what you eat. Baked beans usually contain lots of bacon (or sometimes salt pork) as well as brown sugar, molasses, or maple syrup.

▲▲ Corn pudding. Full of cream and occasionally maple syrup, this is not a side dish for those who are health-conscious.

DELI AND DINER FOOD

●

FEW SMART CHOICES

Salad with mayonnaise

W*hen you're grabbing a quick sandwich to eat at your desk or running out to a coffee shop with friends, are there healthful options?*

TIP

● Salad bars are often priced by weight. If you generally load your container with more than a pound of food, you're probably getting a lot more fat than you bargained for. Heavier foods—such as tuna salads or potato and grain salads—frequently tend to be high in fat or contain high-fat dressings.

Salad sub

WHAT'S IN IT?

Be wary of prepared salads—most are extremely high in fat and can be high in sugars, too. Some roast meats are injected with or marinated in solutions that are high in fat, sugar, or sodium. Opt for house-roasted meats wherever they're offered.

WHAT'S THE BEST?

● Ask for extra vegetables. One lettuce leaf and a slice of tomato won't provide you with many nutrients, but a couple of slices—and maybe some sprouts, too—can help bring you closer to a full serving.

WHAT'S NOT SO GOOD?

● Most sandwiches tend to be overstuffed—they often contain at least 4 ounces of meat but may contain as much as 8 ounces. (For comparison, most supermarket cold cuts list nutrient information for 2-ounce servings.)

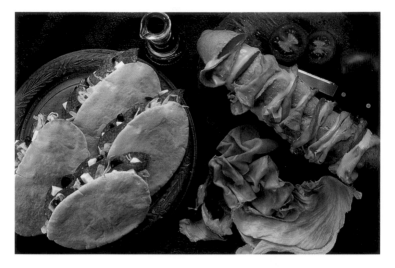

SMART CHOICES

▼▲ The dairy case. Rather than a sugary soda or a high-fat bag of chips, grab a container of juice or milk and a tub of yogurt or an apple. Although juice and flavored yogurts can be high in carbohydrate, they're also substantially higher in vitamins and minerals.

▼ Roast beef. Believe it or not, a roast beef sandwich is almost as good as turkey or chicken. Most delis use lean beef in their sandwiches.

▼▼ Vegetable- and broth-based soups. Research shows that people who start a meal with soup eat fewer calories at that meal than non-soup eaters. Choose a soup that isn't cream-based and one that contains lots of vegetables or whole grains like barley.

Watch out that the sandwiches and pitas you choose aren't overflowing with fillings, mayo—and fat.

NOT-SO-SMART CHOICES

▲▲ Tuna salad sandwich. Tuna's good for you, salad's good for you, so tuna salad must be good for you, right? Wrong—all that mayonnaise makes tuna salad, chicken salad, and egg salads very high in fat. It isn't unusual for the bread to be slathered with even more mayonnaise before the salad's plopped onto it.

▲▲▲ Club sandwiches. Here's a club you won't want to join. This sandwich has three slices of bread, an extra serving of fillings, an extra serving of mayo, and plenty of bacon.

BAR FOOD

●

FEW SMART CHOICES

*Y*ou've met friends after work, and after having a few drinks you all decide you're hungry. What are your options at the bar?

TIP

● Consider having a snack before you go out. Cheese and whole-grain crackers, grapes or oranges, or baby carrots and blue-cheese dip will make a dent in your hunger and can help prevent overeating later.

WHAT'S IN IT?

Most of the options on bar menus emerge from a deep fryer. You'll have to look hard—maybe even on another menu—to find more nutritious offerings.

WHAT'S THE BEST?

● Your best option, believe it or not, may be on the dessert menu: if fresh fruit is offered, order a plate. You'll get some vitamins and fiber, without a lot of fat.

● Some bars set out baskets of peanuts. If you're able to restrain yourself to eating no more than 40 (about an ounce), you'll get beneficial fats, some fiber, protein, and vitamin E.

Grapes

Cheese

Eating some whole-wheat crackers, cheese, and grapes before you go out to eat may take the edge off your appetite.

Whole-wheat crackers

Peanuts

Plain chips

SMART CHOICES

▼ Chips and salsa. Rather than ordering nachos topped with chili, cheese, sour cream, and who knows what else, get a basket of chips—see if baked are an option—and a bowl of salsa.

▼ Buffalo wings. If you're watching your carbs, consider choosing wings (but ask about the sauce, as some are high in sugars).

▼ Plain *quesadillas*. If you can order yours baked instead of fried, you'll cut down considerably on the fat. Still, it's best to split this with a friend or two.

NOT-SO-SMART CHOICES

▲▲▲ Potato skins. They're deep-fried, and then often topped with plenty of cheese, bacon, and sour cream.

▲ Fried anything. Don't be fooled by menu descriptions of "lightly fried" or "lightly battered" foods. Whether it's zucchini sticks, mozzarella sticks, calamari, onion rings, or sweet potato fries, fried foods are not a wise choice.

▲▲ Jalapeño poppers. A variation on *chiles rellenos* made with smaller, hotter peppers, these are stuffed with cheese, then batter-dipped and deep-fried.

WHAT'S NOT SO GOOD?

● If you start feeling hungry, order food before you order another cocktail. Alcohol contains 7 calories per gram (protein and carbs supply 4 calories per gram, fat supplies 9), and it can also lower your inhibitions, making you less aware of how much you are actually eating, when your food finally arrives.

VEGETARIAN

● ● ● ●

MANY HEALTHFUL OPTIONS

With appetizers and entrées inspired by Asian and Middle Eastern cuisines, vegetarian restaurants usually have many nutritious—but not always low-fat or low-carb—offerings.

A dragon bowl of seasonal vegetables, often served with rice or noodles, is a healthful vegetarian option.

WHAT'S IN IT?

Don't panic if you see chicken or fish on the menu at a vegetarian restaurant—it may well be made with soy protein analogs. And if you haven't tried these within the last year or two, try them again. They are improving by leaps and bounds in flavor and texture.

WHAT'S THE BEST?

● Most of the dishes at a vegetarian restaurant will be low in saturated fat, depending on whether dairy and oils containing saturated fats are used. All menu items should be cholesterol-free, though, because cholesterol is only found in animal foods.

soybeans

Tofu with mushrooms and spaghetti.

▼▲ *Edamame*. Fresh soybeans can be roasted and set out as a snack or appetizer, or they can be an ingredient in any number of dishes.

▼▲ Dragon bowl. A mixture of vegetables often depending on the seasons, this dish may also include rice or noodles, as well as tofu.

▼▲ Greek plate. Sometimes called meze or mezze, a platter of Greek appetizers—hummus with pita wedges, *dolmades*, olives, salad greens—can make a delicious meal.

TIP

● If you order a vegetarian entrée at a restaurant that also serves meat, there's a chance that it may not be completely meat-free. Grilled tofu, for example, may be cooked on the same grill as steaks or fish.

NOT-SO-SMART CHOICES

▲▲ Peanut noodles. This dish, sometimes called sesame noodles, contains far more noodles than the recommended serving (sometimes four to six times more), as well as huge quantities of fat.

▲▲ Eggplant. This vegetable acts like a sponge and can absorb several times its own weight in oil. If it's tossed in oil before baking or roasting, or cooked in oil, it can be significantly higher in fat than meat dishes.

▲▲ Burritos. If you find a place that makes a small burrito, you're in luck. These can be high in vitamins and minerals, but portions are often enormous. If yours is, plan to take half home for another meal.

WHAT'S NOT SO GOOD?

● Just because your dish doesn't contain meat, that doesn't mean it will be low-fat! Fats can lurk in dishes where you might not expect them. Roasted veggies are often tossed in generous amounts of oil; pesto and hummus may also contain surprising amounts. Even if they're beneficial fats, it's wise to watch portion sizes.

181

BEVERAGES

BEVERAGES

If you've made healthful choices for your meal, you don't want to blow it by ordering a beverage that contains astonishing amounts of fat or sugars.

The drinks that you choose, whether they are alcoholic or nonalcoholic, caffeinated or herbal tea, or regular or diet soda, can have a considerable effect on your health. The effects, of course, are cumulative, although one or two pina coladas on an occasional basis aren't going to be more harmful to your heart than the occasional platter of barbecued ribs—assuming that you are making healthful food choices most of the time.

SODA, JUICE, WATER, AND TEA

● ● ●

SOME HEALTHFUL OPTIONS

*E*ven healthful "elixirs" and fortified herbal drinks can be high in refined sugars—so be careful what you order.

WHAT'S IN IT?

Did you know that a large soft drink can contain as much as ½ cup of sugar? That includes sweetened teas and bottled juice drinks as well as soda. If you're buying your lunch at a deli, read the labels and avoid anything with "high-fructose corn syrup" as an ingredient.

Cola

TIP

● Juices are usually high in the same nutrients as the foods from which they come. The exceptions to the rule: juices contain less fiber and may contain fewer beneficial compounds known as phytochemicals.

STYLE (1 serving)	CALORIES	CHOLESTEROL mg	SODIUM mg	TOTAL FAT g
12-fl oz soda				
Ginger ale	124	0	26	0
Cola	152	0	15	0
Diet cola	0	0	21	0
8-fl oz juice				
Orange juice	112	0	7	0.3
Cranberry juice cocktail	144	0	5	0.3
Tomato juice	41	0	24	0.1
8-fl oz tea				
Brewed tea	3	0	9	0
Sweetened tea	88	0	8	tr
Snapple Diet Peach Tea	0	0	10	0
Snapple Kiwi-Strawberry	117	0	7	0
Snapple Mango Madness	110	0	10	0
SoBe Pomegranate Cranberry Elixir	100	0	27	0
SoBe Zen Tea	100	0	10	0

Orange and cranberry

WHAT'S THE BEST?

● If you're craving something with a bit more flair than water or club soda, ask for a seltzer with a splash of cranberry or orange juice. It's lower in calories than regular soda, lacks the caffeine of tea, and doesn't have the chemical aftertaste that artificial sweeteners can impart.

WHAT'S NOT SO GOOD?

● Don't order mineral water thinking that you'll get minerals such as calcium, iron, or phosphorus. Yes, the water does contain minerals, but they're measured in parts per million—which means that you get infinitesimal amounts.

SATURATED FAT g	PROTEIN g	CARBOHYDRATE g	FIBER g	SUGARS g
0	0	32	0	32
0	0	38	0	38
0	0	tr	0	0
tr	2	26	0.5	20
tr	0	36	0.3	34
tr	2	10	1	9
0	0	0.9	0	0
0	0.1	22	0	21
0	0	1	0	0
0	0.2	29	0	23
0	0	29	0	27
0	0	26	0	25
0	0	26	0	25

MILK, HOT CHOCOLATE, AND MILK SHAKE

● ● ●

SOME HEALTHFUL OPTIONS

Hot chocolate

*M*ilk is a good source of calcium and provides some protein, but drinks made with milk don't share the nutritional benefits.

WHAT'S IN IT?

When you're at a restaurant, you don't often have a choice between whole, low-fat, or nonfat milk. If you do, though, opt for low-fat. It contains 1 gram of carbohydrate more than whole milk does, but only one-fourth of the fat.

WHAT'S THE BEST?

● Low-fat (or 1 percent) milk is highest in calcium—an 8-fluid ounce glass weighs in with 263 milligrams; the same-size glass of whole milk supplies 246; and nonfat milk has only 223. Chocolate milk (which is usually made with 1 percent milk) has 288 milligrams.

STYLE (8-fl oz serving)	CALORIES	CHOLESTEROL mg	SODIUM mg	TOTAL FAT g
Whole milk	149	34	120	8.2
Nonfat milk	86	5	127	0.4
Low-fat (1%) milk	102	10	124	2.6
Chocolate milk	158	8	153	3
Hot chocolate	113	2	146	1
Shakes (16-fl oz servings)				
McDonald's Chocolate Triple Thick Shake	580	65	280	17
Baskin Robbins Chocolate Shake w/Vanilla Ice Cream & Chocolate Syrup	690	130	210	33
Baskin Robbins Chocolate Shake w/Chocolate Ice Cream	620	105	300	30

I percent milk

Chocolate milk

WHAT'S NOT SO GOOD?

● Although chocolate milk contains slightly more calcium than regular milk, it also has more than twice the carbohydrates. Hot chocolate, which is made from whole milk, contains more fat and more carbohydrate.

● A shake usually contains ice cream and milk, but some contain chocolate or caramel syrup, or are topped with whipped cream. The more you add, the higher the calories and carbs.

SATURATED FAT g	PROTEIN g	CARBOHYDRATE g	FIBER g	SUGARS g
5	8	11	0	11
0.2	8	12	0	12
1.6	8	12	0	12
1.5	8	26	0	26
0,7	2	24	1	21
11	15	94	1	82
21	13	85	0	83
18	15	81	1	77

BEER AND WINE

● ● ●

SOME HEALTHFUL OPTIONS

*I*f you want to have alcohol with your meal, choose a glass of red wine or beer rather than a cocktail, and you'll obtain some health benefits.

Red wine

Beer

Wine and beer both offer modest health benefits when drunk in moderation.

STYLE (12-fl oz serving)	CALORIES	CHOLESTEROL mg	SODIUM mg	TOTAL FAT g
Light beer	99	0	11	0
Low-carb beer	95	0	NA	0
Lager beer	146	0	18	0
Pilsner beer	117	0	14	0.2
Dry red wine (7 fl oz)	148	0	10	0
Dry white wine (7 fl oz)	140	0	10	0
Sweet dessert wine (3.5 fl oz)	165	0	9	0

WHAT'S IN IT?

Beer, wine, and spirits all supply
7 calories per gram. None supplies
significant amounts of nutrients,
although beer provides some B
vitamins and wine contains some iron.

WHAT'S THE BEST?

● Red wine contains flavonoids—
antioxidants that are thought to
increase the levels of beneficial HDL
cholesterol and prevent blood clots.

● Moderation. Experts recommend
no more than one 12-fluid ounce
beer or a 5-fluid ounce glass of wine
per day for women, or twice that for
men, for health benefits.

White wine

TIP

● Alcohol isn't digested; it is
absorbed into the bloodstream
within an hour. Food helps to
slow down the rate at which
the alcohol is absorbed.

WHAT'S NOT SO GOOD?

● Wine glasses come in many
different sizes, and some restaurants
use different shapes for white and red
wine, which can make judging the
amount in a glass difficult. Use a
measuring cup and glass at home
to compare the recommended
5-fluid ounce serving to what you
actually are poured—which is usually
at least 7 fluid ounces.

SATURATED FAT g	PROTEIN g	CARBOHYDRATE g	FIBER g	SUGARS g
0	0.7	4.6	0	0.2
0	0.6	2.6	NA	NA
0	1	13	2	NA
0	1	5.7	0.4	0.2
0	0.4	3.5	0	NA
0	0.2	1.6	0	NA
0	0.2	14	0	8

COCKTAILS

●

FEW HEALTHFUL CHOICES

*D*espite their *"medicinal properties," mixed drinks and cocktails don't have much to recommend them nutritionally.*

TIP

● Higher-proof beverages and sweet liqueurs are higher in calories than lower-proof ones and less-sweet drinks. One fluid ounce of 80-proof whisky, for example, contains 65 calories. The same amount of 100-proof whisky has 83 calories, and a liqueur may have as many as 115 calories per fluid ounce.

WHAT'S IN IT?

Spirits are made by fermenting mash from plants like grain, fruits, or vegetables and then distilling it. Better-flavored liquors are made by steeping a flavoring, such as vanilla beans, in the liquid—a time-consuming process. Inferior ones have flavoring agents, such as vanilla extract or artificial vanillin, added.

WHAT'S THE BEST?

● Gin and vodka are the purest forms of alcohol—that is, they contain fewer adulterants. Flavored vodkas, of course, are either infused with flavorings or have the flavorings added to them.

SMART CHOICES

▼▼ Bloody Mary. This high-flavor cocktail boasts some vitamin C and lycopene, thanks to the tomato juice that it contains.

On-the-rocks. As the ice melts, it dilutes the alcohol, effectively reducing the alcohol content and slowing the rate of absorption.

▲ Fruit juice. If you opt for orange or grapefruit juice, you'll get some vitamin C with your drink; cranberry-juice cocktail and pineapple juice are not-so-smart choices, though, because of their significantly higher sugar content.

NOT-SO-SMART CHOICES

▲▲▲ Pina coladas. Made with the incredibly high-sugar, high-fat cream of coconut, rum, pineapple juice, and sometimes even ice cream, pina coladas can be as high in calories, fat, and carbs as a milk shake.

▲ Mixes. If you order a Margarita, for example, specify that you want it made with tequila, fresh lime juice, and an orange liqueur, rather than from a sour mix. Not only will it taste better, but it will have less sugar and fewer additives.

Inconsistency. Because most drinks are made individually, the actual amounts of liquor and mix can vary each time a drink is poured.

WHAT'S NOT SO GOOD?

● Overindulging. While it's true that a few drinks occasionally might not be harmful to your heart, more than a few drinks in one sitting can affect motor skills, and regular drinking can have a host of negative effects.

Cocktails are fine as an occasional treat, but are often laced with sugar and additives, and are high in fat and carbohydrates.

SPECIAL OCCASIONS

SPECIAL OCCASIONS

Celebrations are often an excuse for relaxing dietary restrictions—and while a slice of cake on your birthday is certainly an acceptable treat, what do you do if you're celebrating someone else's special day? If you're at a wedding reception or a cocktail party that isn't in your honor, are there options that won't derail your healthful-eating plans?

Fortunately, there are nutritious options, but because menus are limited only by a caterer's imagination or a cook's recipe collection, it's hard to be too specific. Here are some general guidelines for you to follow.

BRUNCH

● ● ●

SOME HEALTHFUL OPTIONS

W*hether you're taking the family out to brunch or doing potluck with friends, brunch can be a tricky meal.*

WHAT'S IN IT?

Brunch menus can include anything from quiche and French toast to chicken salad and *penne Bolognese*.

WHAT'S THE BEST?

● The plainer, the better. The more fillings you add to an omelet, the higher in calories it becomes. The same principle applies to salads, sauces, and pancakes.

● Salads, if you choose those made with limited toppings, can be an excellent choice. Or opt for vegetable-based dishes.

Muffins with raspberry jam.

Fruit jams

Plain yogurt

Fried eggs and bacon

Scrambled eggs

WHAT'S NOT SO GOOD?

● Bread baskets. Muffins, croissants, scones, and quick breads are all high in sugar and fat on their own. Add the butter, jam, honey, or honey butter that accompanies them and you're asking for trouble.

SMART CHOICES

Fruit and yogurt. Ideally, you'll be able to opt for plain yogurt—it's highest in calcium, lowest in sugars—and the fruit will include nutrient-dense berries and melons.

Smoked salmon. Go easy on the cream cheese or crème fraîche, and opt for bread or toast rather than a giant bagel.

Granola. Made with whole grains, nuts or seeds, spices like cinnamon, and occasionally dried fruits, this can be a high-fiber option.

NOT-SO-SMART CHOICES

Granola. Sometimes, the grains are roasted in plenty of oil, and sugar, syrup, or fruit juice is added as a sweetener.

French toast. Dipped in an egg-and-milk batter, fried in butter, sprinkled with confectioners' sugar, and then topped with more butter and syrup, this favorite is high in calories, fat, and refined carbohydrates.

Bacon. Not only is this meat extremely high in fat and, usually, sodium, it's also cured with nitrates. When eaten, nitrates convert to nitrites, a potential carcinogen.

WEDDING BUFFETS

●

FEW SMART CHOICES

Wedding receptions may be very simple or extravagantly elaborate—and it's the latter form that presents the challenge to eating healthfully.

TIP

● If you aren't sure whether an item on the buffet fits with your eating plan, ask one of the catering staff. They might not know, but they should be able to find out for you.

Sliced meats

Bite-size hors d'oeuvres make it easy to control portions.

WHAT'S IN IT?

Buffets are known for their astonishing variety. Caterers do realize that guests have a variety of nutritional needs and dietary restrictions, but they're also concerned with flavor—which usually comes in the form of fat and sugar.

WHAT'S THE BEST?

● If the buffet has a carving station, head for it. This will tend to be staffed, and you can tell the carver how small and how lean you'd like your slice of roast meat to be.

● Unless they're drowning in sauce, vegetables are always a safe bet—especially green ones.

Take care not to load your plate too high when you're passing through the buffet.

WHAT'S NOT SO GOOD?

● Most wedding receptions start with hors d'oeuvres. Although these morsels have built-in portion control, they're often very rich. One or two might be acceptable, but it's easy to eat too many. To keep track of how many you've eaten, take a toothpick or napkin with each piece.

NOT-SO-SMART CHOICES

Glistening foods. If you're watching your fat grams, watch out for food that has a sheen to it—it's coated (possibly heavily) in oil.

Use the tip of the serving spoon—don't scoop. Serving spoons often contain 2–4 tablespoons (4 tablespoons is ¼ cup), if filled with liquid to the brim. Remember this when you're helping yourself to that second spoonful of gravy.

Unplanned plates. Plan your plate for maximum nutrition: green food such as salad or vegetables should cover half your plate; protein such as meat or fish should cover a fourth; and starchy vegetables or rice the remaining fourth.

SMART CHOICES

Salmon. Whether it's steamed or roasted, choose this as an entrée and you'll get protein as well as beneficial fats like omega-3 fatty acids. Other fish options are wise choices, too.

Poultry. From the ubiquitous chicken breast to roast duck, poultry is popular, versatile, and lean. As long as it isn't sauced into oblivion or breaded beyond recognition, this is a good choice, whether you're eating low-fat or low-carb.

Get a sense of the options before you pass through the buffet—check to see what you'd really like to eat, and select a few. Take small amounts of those foods, rather than loading your plate with everything that looks appealing.

COCKTAIL PARTIES

●

FEW SMART CHOICES

J ust because cocktail parties tend to be rather brief affairs doesn't mean they can't have a damaging effect on your eating plan.

TIP

● Have a nutritious snack before you go—try baby carrots in blue-cheese or ranch dip. You'll lessen the effects of the alcohol, and the food will take the edge off any hunger pangs if you haven't eaten recently.

Dips make tempting snacks, but try to keep track of how much you're eating and opt for vegetable crudités over chips.

WHAT'S IN IT?

You'll find everything from cheese cubes and miniature wieners to salmon tartare with chive cream at a cocktail party.

WHAT'S THE BEST?

● With flavorsome cocktail snacks, stick with a low-calorie libation. Sparkling water, of course, is the best choice—it's calorie-free, fat-free, and carb-free, but a glass of wine is another good option. Choose red wine and you'll get more antioxidants than you do with white wine.

Nuts contain beneficial fats and protein, and a host of minerals— but pass on very salty ones.

WHAT'S NOT SO GOOD?

● If the food is tasty, it may be all too easy to lose track of how many mini meatballs or egg rolls you've eaten. Allow yourself one trip through the buffet, using the smallest plate available; if the hors d'oeuvres are passed, avoid the fried ones and take a napkin with each so that you know how many you've eaten.

Cashew nuts

Almonds

SMART CHOICES

Olives. Although they're high in sodium, these are also a good source of monounsaturated fats. Choose the pitted variety and you'll be able to keep track of exactly how many you've eaten.

Nuts. Eating nuts on a regular basis can reduce the risk of heart disease. Choose almonds for vitamin E and calcium, cashews for iron and folate, and pistachios for fiber. Skip the Brazil nuts, though—they're quite high in saturated fat.

Vegetables. Much better to choose broccoli florets or red bell-pepper strips as dippers than high-fat, high-carb chips—but better to skip the dip entirely, or to choose a vegetable-based one like hummus or tapenade.

NOT-SO-SMART CHOICES

Pastry. Pass on the mini quiches in tiny pie shells—there's far more crust than filling in a mini quiche— and on anything in puff pastry or phyllo, or mini egg rolls.

Dips. Most dips are based on mayonnaise or sour cream; they are always high in fat and can also be high in saturated fat. It's also impossible to tell how much dip you've actually eaten.

SUMMER BARBECUES AND PICNICS

● ● ●

SOME HEALTHFUL OPTIONS

*S*ummertime, and the living is easy—and, with a little common sense, healthful eating at barbecues and picnics can be pretty easy, too.

Hotdogs with extra onions and condiments add up to a large number of fats and carbs.

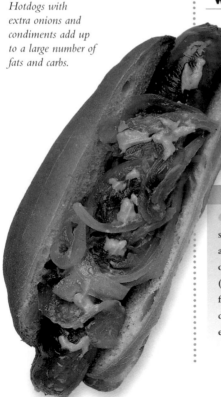

WHAT'S IN IT?

If your summer event is potluck, be sure that what you are offering fits in with your eating plan—know there's at least one safe dish on the buffet.

WHAT'S THE BEST?

● Burgers and chicken are the two safest entrée options. Remove the skin from the chicken if you're concerned about fat (or if it's covered with a sweet sauce and you're limiting your carb intake).

WHAT'S NOT SO GOOD?

● Hotdogs and ribs are two entrées to avoid. Both are extremely high in fat. Depending on the sauce, the ribs may well be high in refined carbohydrate as well. Hotdogs may contain starchy fillers.

TIP

● Grilling is almost synonymous with summer, and that's a good thing. Not only does grilling involve no (or very little) added fat, but fat from the cooking meats can drain off. Just take care not to eat meat that is very charred.

Strawberries

Grapes

SMART CHOICES

Deviled eggs. Even with the mayonnaise and egg-yolk filling, deviled eggs are a pretty good choice. Limit yourself to no more than two halves.

Bean salads. Three- and four-bean salads aren't as popular as they once were, but they are a good source of fiber and, depending on the beans, other nutrients. The dressings may be oily or contain sweetener, so use a slotted spoon if possible.

Fruit salad. If this is in a juice-based dressing rather than a mayonnaise dressing (such as ambrosia), it's low in fat. Go for berries, melon chunks, and red or black grapes for the best nutrition.

NOT-SO-SMART CHOICES

Potato salad. All potato salads are high in carbs; most are high in fat. Don't think that a German-style salad, with it's vinegar-and-mustard dressing, will be a low-fat option. It's often made with bacon and bacon fat or oil. The sauce frequently includes brown sugar, boosting the refined-carb content.

Baked beans. Flavored with bacon or salt pork and brown sugar, molasses, or maple syrup, baked beans are extremely high in carbohydrates and calories.

Coleslaw. If you haven't made a vinegar-based coleslaw at home, you may be surprised to learn that there is often a considerable amount of sugar in the dressing.

HOLIDAY MEALS AWAY FROM HOME

● ● ●

SOME HEALTHFUL OPTIONS

The holiday season is one of festivity, and that often means food—and lots of it. Here's how to manage the main meals, whether at Thanksgiving, Christmas, or any other festival.

Roast turkey

WHAT'S IN IT?

Restaurants and country clubs are often open on holidays, offering a set menu with all the trimmings. Pick and choose carefully, and you'll be able to enjoy a feast that's fairly healthful.

WHAT'S THE BEST?

● Do you have a choice of desserts? If so, go for fresh fruit or for the pumpkin pie. While the latter will never be mistaken for health food, it does provide impressive amounts of vitamin A and iron.

WHAT'S NOT SO GOOD?

● With the exception of turkey, most roasts are high in fat. Prime rib of beef and goose are the worst offenders; leg of lamb and ham are less so. Trim off the fat, remove the skin from poultry or the glaze from ham, and be sure to eat a portion that's about the size of a deck of cards.

SMART CHOICES

Vegetables. Because the meats are often predictably flavored roasts, side dishes are often the best part of a feast. Help yourself to extra Brussels sprouts with roasted chestnuts or mashed rutabaga.

Small portions. Holiday meals are often an excuse to overeat—and with the tremendous variety of foods on most tables, having a little of everything can easily result in a piled-high plate. Keep servings small, and limit yourself to the foods that you really want

NOT-SO-SMART CHOICES

Stuffing. Usually made with sausage, sausage fat, and bread, stuffing is high in fat and carbohydrate. If it's been cooked inside a turkey, there's also a chance that it might harbor harmful bacteria.

Gravy. Before you ladle some onto your meat, take a look at the liquid. Are there small fat globules? Then the pan drippings weren't skimmed properly and the gravy is high in fat. Is it thin and fairly clear, or is it thick and quite opaque? If the latter, it's higher in carbohydrates from flour or starchy thickeners.

Ham and eggs

Before you tuck into your roast beef and gravy, examine the gravy carefully to see if it's been thickened or contains fat globules.

Further Reading

Looking for more information? These pages contain alphabetical lists of books and web sites that you may find helpful.

American Dietetic Association Complete Food and Nutrition Guide
DUYFF, ROBERTA (Wiley, 2002)
Clear explanations of the fundamentals of nutrition, with additional sections for children, women, the elderly, and vegetarians.

Atkins for Life
ATKINS, DR. ROBERT C.
(St. Martin's Press, 2003)
Information on following a controlled-carbohydrate eating plan and making it a way of life rather than a "diet." Includes recipes.

Bowes & Church's Food Values of Portions Commonly Used (17th ed.)
PENNINGTON, JEAN A.T.
(Lippincott-Raven Publishers, 1998)
Nutrient data for thousands of foods, based on an older version of the USDA's Database for Standard Reference, and on information from food companies, trade associations, and scientific literature.

The Complete Book of Food Counts
NETZER, CORINNE T. (Dell, 2000)
Alphabetical listing of nutrient data for packaged foods and fast-food items.

The Food Lover's Companion (3rd ed.)
HERBST, SHARON TYLER
(Barron's Educational Series, 2001)
Definitions and explanations of nearly 6,000 culinary terms.
It's also available online at:
eat.epicurious.com/dictionary/food

The Good Fat, Bad Fat Counter
BUFF, SHEILA
(St. Martin's Press, 2000)
If you're at all confused about trans fats, omega-3s and omega-6s, this little book explains them—and more—clearly and accessibly.

The NutriBase Guide to Fast-Food Nutrition (Avery, 2001)
Part of a series that provides nutrient data for a variety of foods and food groups; this includes information from more than 65 restaurants.

The Nutrition Bible
JEAN ANDERSON, M.S. and
BARBARA DESKINS, PH.D., R.D.
(William Morrow, 1995)
No longer cutting-edge, but solid information nonetheless.

Wellness Foods A to Z
SHELDON MARGEN, M.D. and the Editors of the University of California, Berkeley Wellness Letter (Rebus, 2002)
An A to Z encyclopedia of nutrition information and food facts.

Useful Web Sites

Some restaurant chains provide nutrient breakdowns for menu items on their web sites. Because menus change frequently, it's a good idea to check—it's quite possible that recipes and dishes have changed between this writing and your reading or eating.

Arby's
www.arbys.com

Au Bon Pain
www.aubonpain.com

Baskin-Robbins
www.baskinrobbins.com

Boston Market
www.bostonmarket.com

Burger King
www.burgerking.com

Dairy Queen
www.dairyqueen.com

Denny's
www.dennys.com

Domino's
www.dominos.com

Dunkin Donuts
www.dunkindonuts.com

Haagen-Dazs
www.haagendazs.com

KFC
www.kfc.com

Krispy Kreme
www.krispykreme.com

McDonald's
www.mcdonalds.com

Mrs. Fields
www.mrsfields.com

Olive Garden
www.olivegarden.com

Pizza Hut
www.pizzahut.com

Starbucks
www.starbucks.com

Subway
www.subway.com

Taco Bell
www.tacobell.com

TCBY
www.tcby.com

Wendy's
www.wendys.com

Index

Acknowledgments

Thanks to my favorite dining companions.
Barry, with whom I ate more lunches than I can
remember despite a distance of some 700 miles,
taught me more about food than anyone else.
I share far too few meals with Tom, Amy, Ray,
Anne, and Andy these days, so I treasure the times
we're together. Miguel and Raymond provide love
and laughter at the table and everywhere.